MIROSŁAW SKWIOT
MARIUSZ MOTYKA

THE BATTLESHIPS
SCHARNHORST
AND GNEISENAU

VOL. I

KAGERO

First Edition
© by KAGERO Publishing

AUTHORS
Mirosław Skwiot, Mariusz Motyka

3D VISUALIZATIONS AND DRAWINGS
Mariusz Motyka

PHOTOS
from the archives of Mirosław Skwiot

TRANSLATION/PROOFREADING
Liudmyla Butenko

DTP
KAGERO STUDIO - Łukasz Maj

LUBLIN 2020

ISBN 978-83-66673-15-1

KAGERO Publishing
Akacjowa 100, os. Borek, Turka
20-258 Lublin 62, Poland
phone/fax +48 81 501-21-05
e-mail: kagero@kagero.pl, marketing@kagero.pl
www.kagero.pl, shop.kagero.pl

Table of Contents

*I would like to dedicate this work to my great friend Leszek "Thorr"
Więckowski, with whom we talked for "some time" about the history of the
Kriegsmarine and wrecks sunk in the waters of the Baltic Sea.
Mirosław Zbigniew Skwiot*

Author's note

The battleships of the Kriegsmarine are only four vessels in total, which they managed to put into operational service in 1935-1941. The first two of those, *Scharnhorst* and *Gneisenau*, did not make as spectacular combat career as the other two. So far, no extensive memories of seamen sailing them have appeared, because their career practically boiled down to staying in a port, dock or roadstead until they sank or the hostilities ended. The current publication is a form of compromise between combat operations, shortened in it to a necessary minimum, in the case of *Scharnhorst*, and a broader description of use of the wreck of *Gneisenau* after the war, and a photo album that represents life on the ship. I realise that it is very difficult to show that in several hundred photographs, but the costs associated with the release of such an extensive album were so high that my publisher was unable to bear those in full. Nowadays, without funding of published books, they will have small volume, especially album publications.

There are many places in Poland where, up to the present day, "the remains" of the battleship can be found at workplaces or universities. For me, the most important thing in this publication was to present a new form of stereoscopic photos, which were taken by Dr Wehlau in 1940 and published in an album dedicated to the Kriegsmarine. I managed to purchase those low-volume war-era editions with attached glasses for viewing in 3D and thus present them to a wider audience of readers. The photographs gathered in this album mostly come from my collections, which I bought at bids abroad. They were supplemented with the archives of the late Siegfried Breyer and a few archives from Poland and abroad. The most important of them are the Naval Historical Center in Washington, Imperial War Museum in London and the Archive of Mechanical Documentation in Warsaw. I would also like to thank my friends, who supported me with their collections for this publication: Wawrzyniec Markowski, Mark Twardowski, Mariusz Konarski, Lech Trawicki.

Mirosław Zbigniew Skwiot, Gdańsk 2020

Chapter 1. Designing and constructing the *Scharnhorst* and the *Gneisenau*

The battleship *Scharnhorst* photographed while sailing out for sea tests on April 13, 1939. It is worth paying attention to the mast placed on the funnel in the photo, which was later moved aft.

Introduction

The *Kriegsmarine* battleships, in fact, were only four vessels introduced during 1935-1941. The first two, *Scharnhorst* and *Gneisenau*, were ready before the war and two others, *Bismarck* and *Tirpitz*, were commissioned into the fleet after it had begun. That was the biggest achievement in the arming of the German navy conducted by A. Hitler. Interestingly, all these ships served within the period no longer than a fiscal quarter. If we calculate, it lasted from February to May 1941. In the meantime, *Scharnhorst* and *Gneisenau* were stationed in Brest, France, Bismarck was getting ready for raids on the Atlantic and *Tirpitz* was finishing her sea trials and getting ready for commissioning. *Scharnhorst* and *Gneisenau* had already been through a baptism of fire, which ended with a little victory on the British sea routes. However, staying on the French coast, they constantly were under the threat of air-

strikes. The career of *Bismarck* ended with her sinking though she had successfully attacked British convoys before. As the consequence of that defeat, the German network of sources on the Atlantic was destroyed. Since that moment, raids by heavy German battleships became almost impossible to carry out. Besides, they were suffering from the ever-expanding control of the Atlantic by the Allies. Considering that, *Scharnhorst* and *Gneisenau* escaped to Germany via the English Channel. That bold plan of returning is recognised successful; it became a tactical achievement of Germans but there was a strategic failure behind its apparent excellence and heavy cruisers started being gradually withdrawn from combat operations. The beginning of the end of their military performance was stationing them on the Norwegian waters. Afraid of a potential attack by the Allies, Hitler commanded to deploy battleships and battlecruisers to Norway in order to ensure the supply of ore necessary for manufacturing

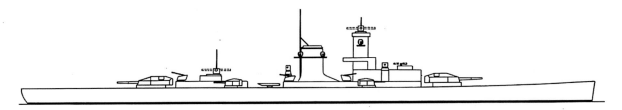

The design of the Panzerschiff D (*Ersatz Elsaß*) developed in 1932 [Drawing by S. Breyer]

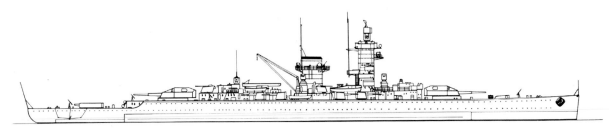

The Panzerschiff C *Admiral Graf Spee*. The first designs of the battleship D were similar to the specifications adopted on the previous units, both in terms of characteristics and side silhouette. The comparison of the two drawings – the design of the battleship D developed in 1932 and the silhouette of *Admiral Graf Spee* – shows it very well. [Drawing by M. Skwiot]

weapons. Before that, *Gneisenau* got attacked and badly damaged, which made her unable to fight almost till the end of the war. In the meantime, *Scharnhorst* and *Tirpitz* remained the only serviceable vessels that could sail to Norway. There they stayed hidden in fjords and were plaguing by the problem of bad fuel supply. After the unsuccessful ending of the Operation *Regenbogen*

in July 1942, Hitler understood that heavy units of the *Kriegsmarine* were unable to fight and he ordered to disengage them. This made Commander-in-Chief Grand Admiral Raeder resign. Although his successor, Dönitz, managed to save most of the ships from getting scrapped, fortune abandoned those units. In 1943, the battlecruiser *Scharnhorst* got sunk by British vessels.

The battleship *Deutschland* photographed on February 27, 1933 during her first voyage in the Nord-Ostsee Canal on her way to the Wilhelmshaven naval shipyard, where the commissioning ceremony was to take place on April 1, 1933.

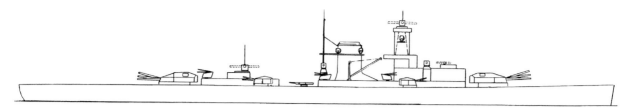

One of the development versions of the battleship D design, dated 1934. [Drawing by S. Breyer]

Tirpitz, the only to remain, sank on 12 November 1944. That was the last ship of its class in the *Kriegsmarine*. The time of heavy ships was irrevocably gone and the history of German battlecruisers ended with that one.

Design

The history of both battlecruisers goes back to the end of 1932. In November, the *Reichsmarine* admiral Raeder met with Reich Minister of Defence, general Groener. During this appointment, they agreed on empowering the future German fleet, which by the end of 1938 featured 6 *Panzerschiffe*, 6 cruisers, 6 destroyers, a flotilla of torpedo boats, 3 flotillas of patrol boats and, in case of the beneficial political situation, 16 U-boats. However, minor difficulties occurred when this ambitious plan was being realised. Construction works on the third unit (*Ersatz Braunschweig*) coincided

with the start of construction the French battlecruiser *Dunkerque*. According to the intelligence information, the estimated displacement of that ship was approximately 26,000 t. Yet the biggest surprise for Germans was its potential speed of 31 kn. If the French armed their vessel with eight 330mm guns, it would become stronger than the *Deutschland*-class units. Suddenly, there was a bad situation for Germans as their ship could be weaker and slower that its prospective adversary. The completed project of the fourth *Panzerschiff 'D'* (*Ersatz Elsaß*) was suspended and its implementation postponed to 1931-1934.

The construction of the battleship 'D' and its prospective characteristics were discussed at several conferences specially organised during 1933. The final requirements were introduced within the discussion held on March 9, 1933. Considering them, three versions of the battleship 'D' project were prepared. The first suggested its displacement constituted 18,000 t,

The commissioning of the French battleship *Dunkerque* changed the previous design of the battleships D and E.

The Panzerschiff *Deutschland*.

the second meant to arm it with 280mm guns and the third one implied the armour comprised of six 330mm guns. Rear admiral Dr. O. Gross, the Commander of the Naval Command Department, endorsed the construction of a battleship displacing 26,000 t and equipped with guns of the calibre 330 mm so it would be close to the French cruiser *Dunkerque*. It was not so easy to

select the right project especially because each of those required a different budget. Basically, constructing a ship displacing 18,000 t cost around 120 million *Reichsmark*. The displacement increase to 22,000 t would require 150 million RM. In its turn, a vessel of 26,000 t would cost 180 million RM. Considering the financial state in the Reich and the threat of its forced disarmament,

The launch of a new battleship named *Tirpitz* on April 1, 1939 was an occasion to conduct a fleet parade at the Wilhelmshaven roadstead. The photo shows *Deutschland* at the roadstead preparing for the side parade of the battleship's crew. There is a He 60 seaplane numbered 60 + D 91 on the catapult of the battleship.

10

infrastructure for her construction and, more importantly, shipbuilding facilities in Germany had to be created. There was also an issue of sea lanes, channels and red military ports unfit for mooring such large units. Apparently, those minor inconveniences fundamentally impacted the characteristics of the future unit. Another factor was the height of the Levensau High Bridge located in the suburbs of Kiel as they viewed the possibility of navigating the ship under it. Considering the stated circumstances, the *Reichsmarine* commander admiral Raeder suggested that several projects of the cruiser were created. Basic requirements included the potential displacement of approximately 26,500 t and armament comprised of 330mm guns. The first version was about to be equipped with four twin-gun turrets, the second one was supposed to have two turrets but each armed with four guns and the third one would have three triple-gun turrets. Referring to the political situation in the German Reich at that time, admiral also commissioned working on a project of a ship displacing 22,000 t and armed with 280mm guns. It was named Project XIII and completed in 1934 so the ship could be laid down the very same year.

the choice appeared hard to made. Another problem were the German shipyards as only the slipway number 2 in Wilhelmshaven was capable of building and launching a ship's hull with the displacement of 26,000 t. Furthermore, docking was only possible at Kaiserdock in Bremenhaven or in Hamburg. Thus, before the battlecruiser 'D' would be built, the appropriate dockyard

However, another conference dedicated to the ship D took place on June 23, 1933. The subject for discussion was the *Deutschland* ship that had already been commissioned into the fleet. The first sea trials revealed her advantages and disadvantages. Considering the information gathered, certain departments of the construction office suggested that changes were made to the ship 'D' project that, incidentally, was primarily based on the ship 'A' project including changes introduced in designing the ship 'C'. All the attendants agreed

The cruiser *Scharnhorst*, the previous unit to bear that name.

The corvette *Gneisenau*, the previous unit to bear that name.

The Panzerschiff *Admiral Scheer*.

The battleship *Elsaß* was to be replaced by *Scharnhorst* after the end of its service.

on thickening the unit's armour. Another subject was prospective armament of the cruisers. The Armaments Department suggested changing the medium weaponry comprised of individual machine guns to two 150mm twin-gun turrets, which they considered better in terms of operating and protection. It was also planned to increase the number of heavy guns of the anti-aircraft battery. Yet all those modernisations needed to be made in a way that the ship with such characteristics would not displace more than 18,000 t. The question of the ship's propulsion system – to use diesel engines or another – was left for the further discussion.

The following conference dedicated to this battleship was held on October 11, 1933. The Armaments Department criticised the suggestion of equipping her with 150mm gun turrets. In particular, they disapproved installation of new barbettes as well as too weak anti-aircraft weapons that was decided to increase from three to four 88mm twin-gun turrets. Within this discussion, the problem of the torpedo armament was also raised but it was less important at that stage of the project development. The most emotional part of the discussion regarded the prospective conning tower, 'komandoturm' – the ship's fore superstructure. The Armaments Department supported the idea of

the cylinder-shaped tower as it had been built for *Deutschland*. But such a construction turned out to be not stable enough in the case it would have to carry fire-control systems, in particular, rangefinders and reticle accessories. A good solution would be moving the turret 'A' closer to the bow and increasing the cubic capacity of the fore superstructure. Thanks to that, the newer and bigger superstructures would become a much more stable platform for the fire-control systems as well as the optical and, prospectively, electrical. The final amendments of the project were related to the increasement of the thickness of armour plates on longitudinal bulkheads. If the mentioned changes were approved, it would be possible to order 280mm gun turrets in November 1933 and 150mm turrets in early January 1934. A week later, on October 18, 1933, it was decided to order two units with the announced displacement of 17,000 t. According to the original documents, the displacement of these battlecruisers was 19,000 t but these figures were crossed and corrected to 17,000 t. After all, this parameter was not so critical as it could be changed in the future because by that moment they had not decided what propulsion system to install, which would increase the displacement of both cruisers.

Admiral Scheer photographed in 1939 after modernisation.

The *Hessen* was to be replaced by *Gneisenau* after the end of her operational service.

Admiral Graf Spee photographed at the roadstead of Port of Wilhelmshaven in the first period of her service.

The battleship *Admiral Graf Spee* photographed under the Levensau High Bridge on the way to Wilhelmshaven base.

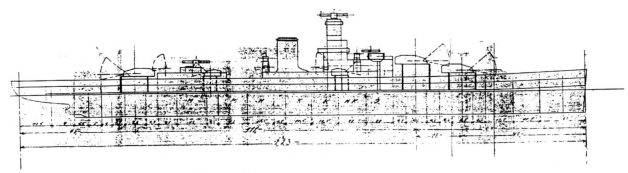

The new design of the battleship D, the so-called *Neuentwurft I*, which was to be armed with 3 gun turrets. [From the collection of S. Breyer]

The battleship *Admiral Graf Spee* photographed in early May 1936 at buoy A 9 in Kiel. The ship's crew are painting the vessel before the fleet parade planned for the end of May.

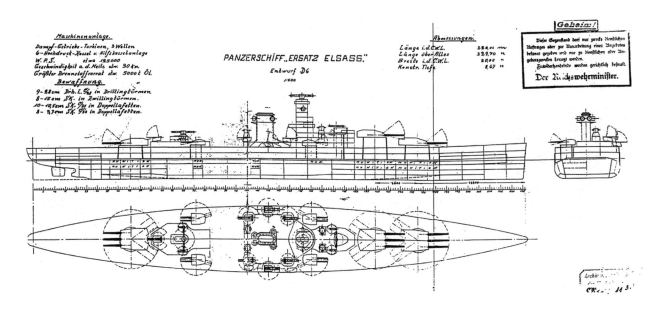

One of the versions of the Panzerschiffe D (*Ersatz Elsaß*) design – the *Entwurf D6* – providing it with nine SK C/28 guns with a caliber of 28 cm placed in 3 gun turrets. [From the collection of S. Breyer]

18

The question of the calibre of the main battery was raised again in December 1933. Within the yearly budget, they set a quota of 1,4 million RM for manufacturing new 330mm guns. However, the political situation in Germany required to reduce their calibre to 305 mm. The Armaments Department estimated the production time and concluded that the works on the gun turrets would take almost a year and their building would continue within next 3,5 years. Thus, construction of battleships with the displacement of 25,000 t

Equipping work on the battleship *Scharnhorst* in the summer of 1937. In the foreground, we can see the ship's turret A covered with tarpaulin. In the background, the assembly of the first tier of the bow superstructure and the command post began. Further, we can see the tower C completed.

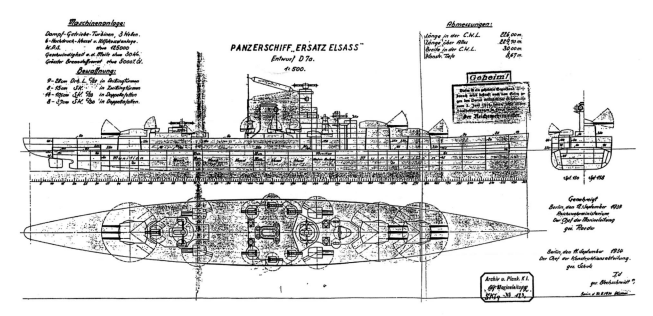

The design of the Panzerschiffe D (*Ersatz Elsaß*) – the Entwurf D7a – approved on September 12 by Admiral Raeder. Based on this design, the battleships D and E were built, and the main constructor of both ships, Blechschmidt, supervised it. [From the collection of S. Breyer]

The ceremony of launching the hull of the battleship *Gneisenau*.

and their armament of six 305mm guns would start by 1935-1936. Considering the political situation in 1936, when the mandatory disarmament treaties were to be expired, starting the construction of the units in 1935 would allow Germany to save a year in the cycle of building and equipment. In December 1933, A.

Hitler met with the Fleet Commander, admiral Raeder, and authorised building the fourth unit, so-called battlecruiser 'D', within the budget for 1934. Raeder also received the permission for building the fifth one, *Panzerschiff 'E'* – *Ersatz Hessen*. At that appointment, the admiral presented the project on increasement of the

The moment the *Gneisenau's* hull is hitting the quay.

future ships' combat value in comparison to *Deutschland*. In the end, he was not able to convince Hitler. On the other hand, the latter approved the suggestion of reinforcing the ships' armour, which would increase their displacement to 19,000 t, yet did not agree to add the

third 280mm gun turret. The order for both units was issued on January 25, 1934: the battleship 'D' (*Ersatz Elsaß*) was to be built at the Wilhelmshaven shipyard and the battleship 'E' (*Ersatz Hessen*) at the Deutsche Werke shipyard in Kiel. The project submitted to the

The Chancellor of the Third Reich A. Hitler took part in the launching ceremony of *Scharnhorst*.

Ceremony for launching the hull of the battleship *Scharnhorst*. On the honorary stand, we can see guests invited along with the battleship's godmother.

Launching the hull of the battleship
Scharnhorst.

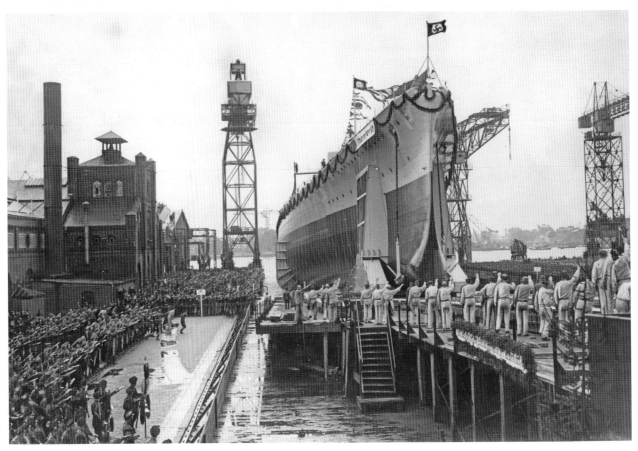

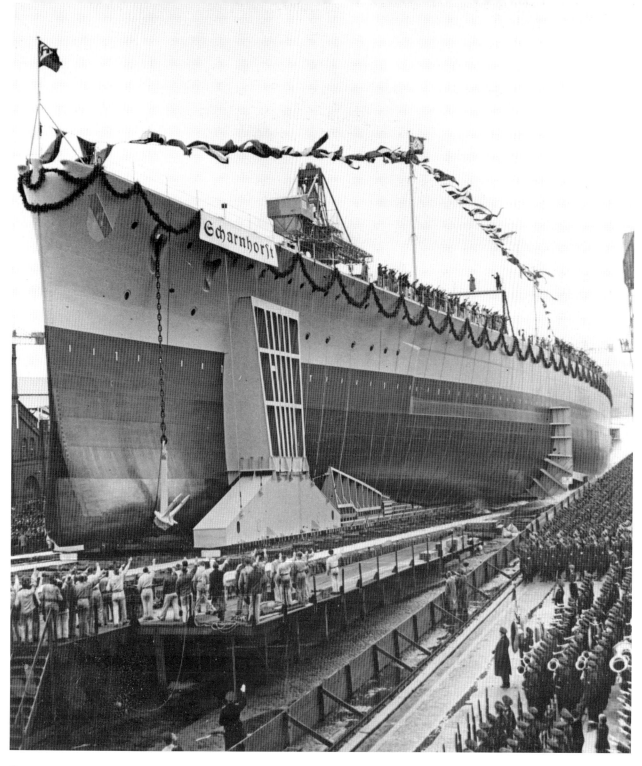

The hull of the battleship *Scharnhorst* slides off the ramp into the water after the stoppers have been released.

The *Scharnhorst's* hull is towed away safely to the equipment wharf.

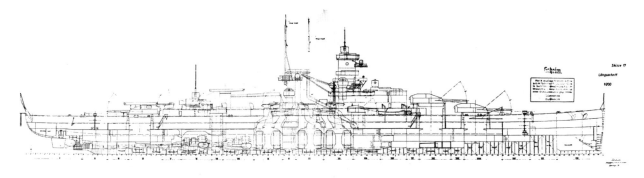

Longitudinal drawing of the cross-section of the battleship *Gneisenau* [The collection of S. Breyer]

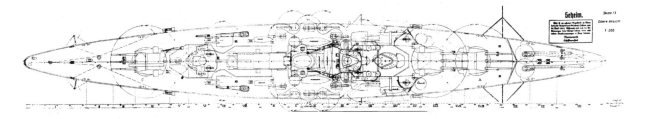

Drawing – the top view – of the battleship *Gneisenau* [The collection of S. Breyer]

The battleship *Gneisenau* departing from Kiel for her first sea trials, photographed in early April 1938.

The battleship *Gneisenau*, after leaving the roadstead in Heikendorf, passes Möltenort on her way to the Bay of Kiel, where it will undergo sea trials. The plan included mainly tests of the main engines and boiler equipment. The photo of the battleship was taken in late April or early May 1938, even before she was officially put into service.

The battleship *Gneisenau* sets out for speed tests scheduled to be performed on the waters of the Bay of Kiel.

shipyards presented units displacing 18,000 t and armed with two 280mm triple-gun turrets, four 150mm twin-gun turrets and four 88mm twin-gun turrets. The actual information on those units is given in the table 1. Both cruisers were laid down on February 14, 1934.

Tab. 1. Parametres of the D and E cruisers introduced in projects approved in 1932-1934

No.	Parametre	
1.	Designated displacement	approx. 23,000 t
2.	Standard displacement	approx. 19,700 t (19,400 short tons)
3.	Length	207,00 (209,70) m
4.	Beam	25,60 m
5.	Draught	7,71 m
6.	Propulsion	Diesel Engines MAN 12-cylinder M 12 Z 42/58 10 625 HP (in total 85,000 HP)
7.	Speed	26 kn (with diesel engines 28 kn)
8.	Armament	6 x 28 cm (2 x III); 8 x 15 cm (4 x II); 10 x 10,5 cm (5 x II); 8 x 3,7 cm (4 x II)
9.	Torpedo tubes	8 (2 x IV)
10.	Armour	
	Belt	220 mm
	Citadel	35mm side, 60mm face, 80mm rear, 40mm roof
	Superstructure deck	45 mm
	Armoured deck	40 mm
	Armoured deck above the engine room	80 mm
	Torpedo bulkheads	45 mm
	Barbettes of the main battery	220 mm
	Command post	300 mm

When building of units number 235 and 125 started at the German shipyards, admiral Raeder was not satisfied with their construction. In his opinion, these ships were built under the pressure of the political situation that was not beneficial for Germans then. Additionally, they might be weaker than their potential adversary, *Dunkerque*. According to him and the overwhelming majority of senior German officers, the 'E' and 'D' ships could have a chance after the installation of the third

gun turret, 280 mm in height, that Raeder strongly insisted on. He came to this decision during the appointment with Hitler on June 27, 1934. In fact, he agreed on building the third turret but spoke against increasing the calibre of guns. Adding the third turret suspended further building of the ships because its installation would require construction changes in the entire project. Working on both units stopped on July 5, 1934. In the meantime, the Armaments Department estimated that new technical drawings for the battleship would be finished by October 1935 the fastest. The situation with subcontractors and equipment seemed a little worse as they worked with little delays. In addition, correcting the project along with the orders for materials postponed the initial date of launching the ships for the indefinite period of time.

The following day, on July 6, 1934, the conference on remodelling the ship 'D' project was organised. The Navy Office supported the variant with placing one fore turret and two aft turrets and preserving the constant speed of 28 kn and maximum speed of 30 kn. The armour had to withstand the impact of a 330mm shell fired from the distance of 15,000-20,000 metres. Besides, they required the belt armour to be 300-350mm thick and wanted to armour the citadel, bow and stern. The battlecruiser was not intended to have either torpedo or air equipment. In its turn, the lack of the detailed intelligence information about the thickness of *Dunkerque*'s belt armour became the reason to postpone the final decision on the calibre of the main battery guns that were initially supposed to be 280 mm. The offer to arm the unit with 330mm twin-gun turrets was rejected since working on those and constructing and installing them would only make it possible to launch the ship in the middle of 1939. After all, the problem of armament did not aggravate as there was an option of its later turning

The battleship *Scharnhorst* moored in the port of Wilhelmshaven, just before she was officially put into service. The ceremony took place on January 7, 1939, and her first commander was Commander Otto Ciliax.

Both battleships, *Scharnhorst* and *Gneisenau* photographed on the waters of Kiel in April or May 1939. In the foreground, Scharnhorst still has a straight stem before reconstruction, and Gneisenau (on the right) already has a new stem and funnel cover.

The battleship *Gneisenau* photographed during the great parade of the fleet on August 22, 1938.

The battleship *Gneisenau* photographed after the parade, on the way to Kiel. The peculiarity of this photo is the removed (retouched) flag of the regent of Hungary, Admiral M. Horthy de Nagybánya, on the battleship's mast.

The battleship *Gneisenau* moored to the buoy A8 at the Heikendorf roadstead in Kiel. This picture was taken right after the launch of the heavy cruiser *Prinz Eugen* in late August 1938.

The photo of the battleship *Gneisenau* anchored at the Heikendorf roadstead, taken in the spring of 1939 in Kiel. As you can see, the ship has a new stem. As it soon turned out, this configuration of the main anchors did not work, and the ship had to undergo the reconstruction of her stem again. This time she received a more slanted one and the position of the anchors was changed: those were placed in the bow half-hawseholes.

into gun turrets mounted within 9 months. The most problematic part was the unit's propulsion system that had not been chosen by that time. Two variants were reviewed: the first one featuring a steam turbine and the second one with turbo-electric transmission. The matter of installing diesel engines was definitely rejected because of their heaviness. The new projects of the battleships were named *Neuentwurft I* and *Neuentwurft II* (from German: New Project I and New Project II); all the details are presented in the table 2.

Tab. 2. Technical data of the projects approved on 19 June 1934

No.	Parametre	Neuentwurft I	Neuentwurft II
1.	Designated displacement	33,400 t	30,950 t
2.	Standard displacement	30,400 short tons	28,000 short tons
3.	Length	227,00 m	223,00 m
4.	Beam	30,00 m	29,30 m
5.	Draught	8,70 m	8,40 m
6.	Propulsion	Turbines	Turbines
7.	Power	125,000 SHP	105,000 SHP
8.	Speed	30 kn	28 kn
9.	Number of shafts	3	3
10.	Armament	9 x 18 cm (3 x III); 8 x 15 cm (4 x II); 10 x 10,5 cm (5 x II)	9 x 28 cm (3 x III); 8 x 15 cm (4 x II); 10 x 10,5 cm (5 x II)
11.	Torpedo tubes	No	No
12.	Armour		
	Belt	350 mm	300 mm
	Citadel	60mm face, 90mm rear	60mm face, 90mm rear
	Superstructure deck	50 mm	50 mm
	Armoured deck	60-100 mm	60-100 mm
	Barbettes of the main battery	350 mm	350 mm
	Command post	350 mm	350 mm

When all the details were arranged and approved, it might seem that the construction of the cruisers would start instantly. Yet the problem of choosing the propulsion system and the main armament stood in the way. Regarding the first matter, they reviewed two kinds of propulsion: diesel engines and high pressure turbines operating with superheated steam. After studying the experience of exploiting diesel engines on *Deutschland* or *Bremse*, it was concluded that these devices caused quite many troubles. Likewise, they turned out to be heavier than steam turbines because of their size so as they had to keep the displacement limit, turbines were the better option. Consequently, admiral Raeder commissioned fulfillment of other versions of the project based on original *Neuentwurft II*; those were named from D1 to D7 and featured different configurations of anti-aircraft weapons. Besides, he rejected the offer featuring diesel engines and endorsed the variant with steam turbines. As for the second question, they got back to the discussion in March 1935. Five versions of the main armament were introduced:

a. nine 305mm guns arranged in 3 triple-gun turrets;
b. nine 330mm guns arranged in 3 triple-gun turrets;
c. nine 380mm guns arranged in 2 triple-gun turrets;
d. nine 330mm guns arranged in 2 triple-gun turrets;
e. nine 350mm guns arranged in 2 triple-gun turrets.

According to the first three versions (a, b, c), the estimated displacement was 34,000-37,000 t. Working on the project of such gun turrets would take approximately 1,5 years. Together with the estimated time of 3,5 years needed to construct and equip them, the total duration would be nearly 5 years! So if the construction

The battleship *Gneisenau* photographed at the roadstead in Wilhelmshaven in spring 1939.

The turret B and the bow superstructure of the battleship *Gneisenau* photographed in early 1940 during the voyage to the Bay of Kiel.

of the ship had started in 1935, it would only have been possible to launch her in 1940. Among the rest versions, the armament configuration 'd' turned out to be the most sufficient as it allowed to complete the cruiser 'D' within 16-17 months. As for the cruiser 'E', it would take a little longer – 22-23 months respectively. However, if they chose that version, it would cost them 11 million RM to commence works and build turrets and 280mm guns. This offer was hard to accept in terms of financing. As an alternative, it was possible to modify the battleship with 350mm guns later; mounting those would increase the displacement of 650 t and the estimated draught of 15

Sailors handling auxiliary devices inside the engine room of the battleship *Scharnhorst*.

Sailors handling auxiliary devices inside the engine room of the battleship *Scharnhorst*.

Sailors handling the engine room of the battleship *Gneisenau*.

A sailor handling the boilers.

A sailor passing above the turbine of the battleship *Scharnhorst*.

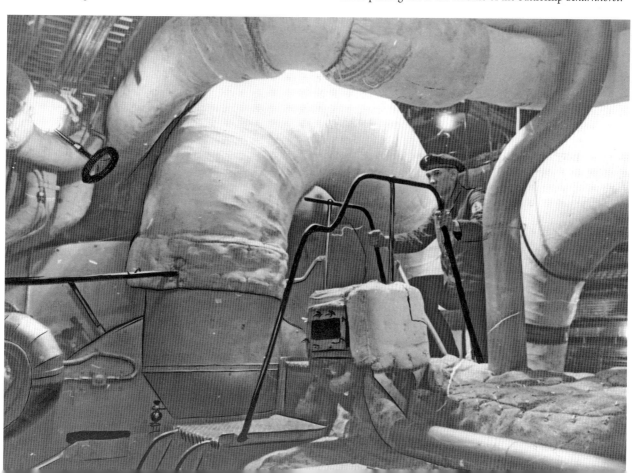

Bow turrets of the main battery of the battle-ship *Gneisenau*. In the background, on the left side of the photo, you can see the battleship *Scharnhorst* with a new mast at the stern.

Bow turrets of the main battery of the battle-ship *Gneisenau*.

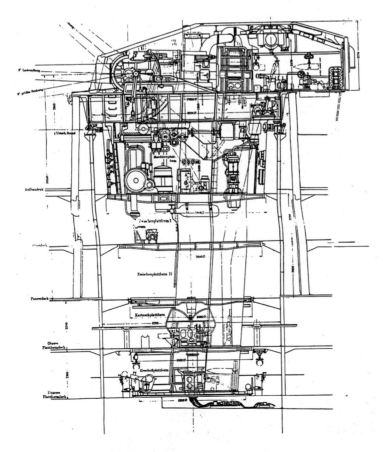

A cross-section of a 28cm gun turret.

The funnel of the battleship *Gneisenau* with its mast seen from the aft hangar deck. The photo was taken after the installation of the radar, which is visible in the photo behind the curtain of black smoke coming from the funnel. The photo was probably taken in November 1939, during a joint raid with *Scharnhorst* under the command of Vice Admiral Marschall, who took over the position of Fleet Commander after Admiral Boehm.

centimetres. Such parameters were acceptable as they did not have any big impact on steering or docking the ships as well as navigating them through locks and canals. The only problem with changing the calibre was the amount of ammunition they could store in magazines. If the calibre was 280 mm, they could allocate 150 missiles per each gun, while for a 350mm gun that would be 130 missiles. The bigger the calibre was, the longer the firing distance would become. Furthermore, that would enable penetrating the side armour of *Dunkerque*. In the light of those facts, it was not as easy to choose the calibre of

the main weapons as it seemed in the beginning. Each variant had its benefits and downsides. The armament of the ships 'D' and 'E' was a compromise between the financial and political situations in Germany. The order was to arm the units with 280mm triple-gun turrets that soon could be replaced with 350mm guns. Later, it turned out that 350mm guns were a little weaker than more efficient 330mm ones. Eventually, the matter of modifying the ships was left for the further discussion.

The German policy considerably changed in early 1935. On March 16, the Chancellor of Germany A.

Hitler commanded to disregard the decrees of the Treaty of Versailles. As a consequence of the rapid diplomatic intervention of the British, the mutual maritime agreement was signed on June 18, 1935; it gave Germany the proportion of 35% in comparison to the Royal Navy fleet. After the recalculation, the granted limit in the battleship category was approximately 83,000 t. That agreement did not have an impact on the ships 'D' and 'E' under construction since they had been laid down on June 15, 1935 at the Kriegsmarinewerft shipyard in Wilhelmshaven and on May 6, 1935 at the Deutsche Werke shipyard in Kiel.

Construction of *Scharnhorst* and *Gneisenau*

The contract for the battleship 'D' *Ersatz Elsaß* was awarded to the Kriegsmarinewerft shipyard in Wilhelmshaven on January 25, 1934. The construction started on February 14, 1934 with laying her keel on the slipway number 2. However, new circumstances occurred in the process of further building and suspended the progress. They need to be mentioned again. Within the meeting that took place on June 5, 1934 the Chancellor of Germany approved implementation of the third gun turret. That decision halted the building of both battleships. The installation of new turrets required construction changes in the entire project. Making these changes along with correcting the orders for building materials postponed the initial date of launching the units for the period that was hard to define then. The following day, on June 6, 1934, the conference on changing the project of the battleship 'D' was gathered. The Navy Office supported the offer of placing one turret on the bow and two on the stern as well as keeping the constant speed of 28 kn and maximum speed of 30 kn. The armour had to withstand the impact of a 330mm shell fired from 15,000-20,000 m. They also required her belt armour to be 300-350 mm thick and her citadel, bow and stern to be armoured. Lacking the detailed intelligence information about the thickness of *Dunkerque*'s belt, they had to put aside the issue of the calibre of the main battery, which was initially meant to be 280 mm. The offer to equip the battleship with 330mm twin-gun turrets was rejected since with building and installing those would postpone the ship's commissioning to the middle of 1939. Yet the problem of armament was not solved immediately as there was the possibility to later transform it into gun turrets that could be mounted in

9 months. The battleship's keel was repeatedly laid on June 15, 1935 at Kriegsmarinewerft in Wilhelmshaven[1]. The hull launching took place on October 3, 1936; her godmother became the widow of Commander Feliks Schultz, the CO of the armoured cruiser *Scharnhorst* sunk in the Battle of the Falkland Islands.

The contract for the battleship 'E' *Ersatz Hessen* was signed on January 25, 1934 with the Deutsche Werke shipyard in Kiel. They laid her down on February 14, 1934 yet the further works were suspended on July 5, 1934 and the slipway was cleaned. The hull fragments were actually removed from it. However, more importantly, the contract itself remained valid and the construction would continue as soon as the modified project was accepted. As we know, the key decision to add the third gun turret was made on June 27, 1934 and that halted the construction for a while. Along with this, the calibre of the main battery remained 28 cm. That decision was only made to avoid greater delays. Additionally, they preserved the opportunity to redesign the battleship in the future. During the projection, it was recommended that they select barbettes on which turrets with guns of a larger calibre (330, 350 or 380 mm) could be mounted. The estimated duration of such works was approximately 12-15 months. Changing the number of the main weapons led to changing the class of the units from *Panzerschiffe* (armoured ships) to *Schlachtschiffe* (battleships). Officially, the keel was repeatedly laid on July 6, 1935. The hull was launched on December 8, 1936 and Colonel General of the German Army Freiherr von Fritsch made the christening speech. Her godmother became the widow of Julius Markerz, the commander of the armoured cruiser *Gneisenau*. The ceremonial launching was accompanied by a little incident: because of the mechanical failure, they could not completely stop the floating hull and it hit the wall of the Hindenburg Embankment opposite. Luckily for the vessel, only the wharf but not her hull got damaged. The equipment works continued as planned and the ceremony of commissioning the ship into the *Kriegsmarine* was held on May 21, 1938. F. Förster, the former CO of the light cruiser *Karlsruhe*, took the command of her. Also, a large proportion of the first *Gneisenau*'s crew came from that unit. Lieutenant commander Schonemark, the executive officer on *Gneisenau*, had previously been the head of the team of specialists

---

[1] The construction of *Scharnhorst* lasted for 42 months and cost 143,471 mln RM; for *Gneisenau* it took 37 months and cost 146,174 mln RM.

The stern turret of the main battery of the battleship *Scharnhorst* with a catapult on the turret's roof. This photo was taken while the vessel was in dock.

Bow turrets of the main battery of the battleship *Gneisenau*. In the background, on the left side of the photo, you can see the battleship *Scharnhorst* with a new mast at the stern and a new bow.

The stern tower of the main battery of the battleship *Gneisenau* with a catapult mounted on its roof, photographed during the vessel's stay in dock.

An Arado Ar 196 seaplane mounted on the catapult of the battleship *Gneisenau*.

who built and equipped her. On the day of commissioning, the crew comprised 1,700 people.

The hull and the engine room

In construction of the battleships, they used the standard transverse and longitudinal layout of the hull braces. Individual web frames were installed at distances varying between 0,75 m and 1,5 m depending on the area of their mounting: starting in the aft section, throughout the midship and farther towards the bow. The hull was divided lengthwise into 21 integral watertight compartments each marked with Roman numerals from I to XXI. Inside the ship, individual

compartments had appropriate markings on their walls, which helped the crew orientate. Every compartment featured an autonomous damage control system integrated with the main control unit as well as auxiliary units. Inside the hull, there was the armoured citadel protecting all the vital components such as the engine room, magazines and barbettes. For the hull, they used new St 42 and 52 KM shipbuilding steel. Propulsion of both battleships was meant to include high pressure turbines supplied by superheated steam. *Scharnhorst* received 3 sets of Brown Boveri turbines using steam generated by 12 high-pressure Wagner boilers manufactured by Deschimag A.G., Bremen. In the course of sea trials, she reached the maximum speed of 31,65 kn with the power output of 161,800 HP. *Gneisenau* was equipped with 3 sets of Deschimag A.G. turbines each providing 53,350 SHP. They were also powered by steam coming from 12 high-pressure boilers of the same kind. During sea trials, the ship reached the maximum speed of 30,7 kn with the power output of 151,900 HP. Her range at the maximum speed was 2,900 nautical miles, 6,200 NM at the speed of 19 kn and 8,380 NM at the speed of 15 kn. For *Scharnhorst*, these values constituted respectively 2,210 NM, 7,100 NM and 9,020 NM. The energy supply for electrical devices was generated by 5 power stations located in 4 compartments. There were 4 diesel generators and 8 turbogenerators producing in total 4,120 kW at 220 V DC.

Tabl. 3. General characteristics

No.	Parametre	Gneisenau	Scharnhorst
1.	Designated displacement	38,100 t	37,822 t (1935) / 38,700 t (1943)
2.	Standard displacement	35,500 t	31,552 t (1935) / 32,358 t (1943)
3.	Length	226,00 m /overall 229,80 m*	226,00 m
4.	Beam	30,00 m	30,00 m
5.	Draught	9,9 m	8,69 m (1935) / 9,9 m (1943)
6.	Propulsion	3 Deschimag A.G. turbines 12 Wagner boilers	3 Brown Boveri turbines 12 Wagner boilers
7.	Power	151,900 HP	160,050 SHP
8.	Speed	31,65 kn	31,00 kn
9.	Armament: main battery	9 x 28 cm SK C/34 (3 x III)	9 x 28 cm SK C/34 (3 x III)
	Secondary battery	12 x 15 cm SK C/28 (4 x II, 4 x I)	12 x 15 cm SK C/28 (4 x II, 4 x I)
	Anti-aircraft battery	14 x 10,5 cm SK C/31 |(7 x II)	14 x 10,5 cm SK C/31 (7 x II)
		16 x 3,7 cm SK C/30 (8 x II)	16 x 3,7 cm SK C/30 (8 x II)
		10 x 2 cm SK C/30 (10 x I)	10 x 2 cm SK C/30 (10 x I)
	Torpedo tubes	6 x 53,3 cm (2 x III, 18 torpedoes)	6 x 53,3 cm (2 x III, 18 torpedoes)
10.	Seaplanes	1 – 3 Ar196A1 – A3	1 – 3 Ar196A1 – A3
11.	Crew	56 officers 1,613 NCOs and seafarers (1935)	60 officers 1,908 NCOs and seafarers (1943)

*234,9 m upon remodelling

Armour

The *Scharnhorst*-class battlecruisers were the first *Kriegsmarine* units for which they widely used new armour materials – hard Wotan (German: Wotan hart, abbreviated as Wh) and soft Wotan (Wotan weich, or Ww) steel. Those replaced nickel steel plates commonly used for the previous *Deutschland*-class ships as well

as Krupp KNC (Krupp Non-Cemented) steel. Thanks to the special welding technology, the new materials allowed producing thicker yet lighter armour. They were primarily used for making 50-150mm armoured plates. The remaining armour was made of face hardened steel (Krupp Cementiert Panzer, or Krupp Cemented Armour) that could be welded. The main armoured belt covered both sides between the frames 32 and 185,7; it extended from 1,7 m below the waterline to 3 m above it. Amidships, its thickness was 170 mm below the waterline and 350 mm above it. In the bow area, it tapered to 70 mm and 150 mm respectively, while in the stern area it was 170 mm and 200 mm. The anti-splinter layer stretched above the belt armour. It was made of Wh and its thickness was 40-45 mm in the citadel area and 35 mm in both forward and aft sections. Longitudinal bulkheads provided internal protection. The torpedo bulkhead stretched between the frames 32 and 185,7 was made of 45mm Ww. Horizontal protection comprised two decks: an upper and an armoured one. The upper deck was made of 50mm Wh and stretched above the entire hull. The armoured deck, made of 80-95mm Wh, extended between the front and aft armoured bulkheads (between the frames 10,5 and 185,7). The battleship had three transverse armoured bulkheads: one front and two rear. The 150mm front bulkhead was mounted at the edge of the belt, near the frame 185,7. Likewise, the rear bulkhead, made of a 200mm Krupp steel plate, was mounted near the frame 32. The last one, also 150mm thick, was installed right behind the ship's steering gear. The thickness of the main battery armour varied between 90 and 360 mm in different sections. The turret fronts were protected with 360mm armour as well as 150mm sloped plates. 150-220mm^2 armour was plated on their sides, while their rears were covered with 350mm armour also ensuring their balance. Their roofs were made of 180mm armour plates. For all that armour, they used Krupp steel.

Armament

The main battery comprised 9 quick-firing SK C/34 guns of the calibre 28 cm manufactured by Krupp Arms Works. Designed for *Scharnhorst* and *Gneisenau*, guns of that model had the actual calibre of 283 mm and were arranged in triple Drh L C/28 turrets. In comparison to the previous version of 28cm guns, C/34 fired

---

[2] Different sources in German provide controversial data.

The funnel of the battleship *Scharnhorst.*

more elongated projectiles yet preserved the same propellant charges. The extra weight of projectiles, ensured by warheads of a new type, allowed piercing armour plates with higher effectiveness. When her career just started, *Gneisenau* had a catapult on her turret 'C', which would considerably reduce her maneuvering speed. Therefore, that catapult was dismounted in February 1940. When the ship was disarmed in the middle of 1942, her turrets 'D' and 'C' were prepared for transportation to Norway in order to reinforce the local coastal defense system. The secondary battery included twelve 150mm SK C/28 guns arranged in four single open MPLC/28 mounts and four twin LC/34 turrets. The characteristics of 28cm and 15cm guns are given in the table 4.

The heavy anti-aircraft battery of the ships consisted of fourteen quick-firing 10,5cm SK C/33 guns placed in twin LC 31 gE mounts. They were arranged as follows: 6 open mounts on the lower level of the fore superstructure near the funnel and one on the aft superstructure in front of the turret 'C'. The medium anti-aircraft battery of the had sixteen 37mm guns fixed in eight twin C/30 mounts. Four mounts were on the lower superstructure deck right behind the turret 'B'. Another four mounts were installed on both sides of the aft fire control post, also on the superstructure level. The brief characteristic of the heavy and medium anti-aircraft guns is given in the table 5.

Tab. 4. General characteristics of 28 cm SK C/34 guns and 15 cm SK C/28 guns

No	Parametre	SK C/34	SK C/28
1.	Calibre	283 mm	149,1 mm
2.	Weight	53,25 t	9 026/9 080 kg
3.	Overall length	15,415 mm	8,200 mm
4.	Length of the barrel	14,505 mm	7,816 mm
5.	Length of the chamber	2,619 mm	1,152 mm
6.	Chamber capacity	180 dm^3	21,7 dm^3
7.	Length of the driving band	11,725 mm	6,588 mm
8.	Number of grooves	80 (3,25 mm x 6,72 mm)	44 (1,7 x 6,14 mm)
9.	Weight of a shell	330 kg	45,3 kg
10.	Propellants	119 kg RP C/38 (15/4,9)	14,15 kg RPC/38 (7,5/3)
11.	Muzzle velocity	890 m/s	875 m/s
12.	Working pressure	3,200 kg/cm^2	3,000 kg/cm^2
13.	Effective operation time	300 shots	1,100 shots
14.	Maximum range	40,930 m / 40°	22,000 m / 35° 23,000 m / 40°

Tab. 5. General characteristics of 10,5 cm SK C/33 guns and 3,7 cm SK C/30 guns

No	Parametre	SK C/33	SK C/30
1.	Calibre	150 mm	37 mm
2.	Weight	4,560 kg	243 kg
3.	Overall length	6,840 mm	3,074 mm
4.	Length of the barrel	6,348 mm	2,960 mm
5.	Length of the driving band	5,531 mm	2,554 mm
6.	Number of grooves	36 (1,3 x 5,5 mm)	16 (0,55 x 4,76 mm)
7.	Projectile weight	15,1 kg	0,748 kg
8.	Propellants	6,05 kg RPC/40 N (5,5/2,1)	0,365 kg RPC/38 N
9.	Muzzle velocity	900 m/s	1000 m/s
10.	Working pressure	2,850 kg/cm^2	2,950 kg/cm^2
11.	Effective operation time	2,950 shots	7,500 shots
12.	Maximum range	17,700 m	8,500 kg / +35,7°
13.	Maximum elevation	12,500 m / +80°	6,800 m / +85°
14.	Loading speed	15 shots/min	30 shots/min

The light anti-aircraft battery was comprised of ten single 20 mm MG C/30 guns. At the beginning

An Arado A 196 A1 seaplane with civilian numbers on the catapult of turret C of the battleship *Gneisenau*.

Cleaning of the deck by sailors from the battleship *Gneisenau*. In the foreground, the 15cm gun turrets are visible.

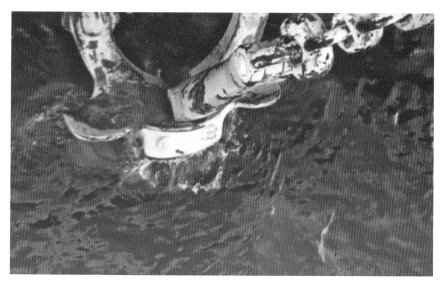

Lifting one of the anchors of the battleship *Gneisenau*.

of 1940, they changed the model to MG C/38. The number of anti-aircraft weapons regularly changed during the entire ships' service history.

Tab. 6. General characteristics of 2cm MG C/30 guns

No	Parametre	
1.	Overall length	2,300 mm
2.	Length of the barrel	1,300 mm
3.	Length of the chamber	140,6 mm
4.	Rifling length	1,159.4 mm
5.	Number of grooves	8
6.	Rifling length (calibres)	36 calibres
7.	Maximum elevation angle	+85°
8.	Minimum depression angle	-10°

In the summer of 1941, both ships stationed in Brest were equipped with 2 triple-torpedo tubes of the calibre 533 mm, which had previously been dismounted from light cruisers. Hence, *Gneisenau* received those from *Leipzig* and *Scharnhorst* from *Nürnberg*. Each ship received 18 torpedoes.

Equipment

The optical fire-control system was comprised of two 10,5m rangefinders, one located atop the fore superstructure and another at the aft command post. Each of them was mounted on a rotary, gyro-stabilised armoured turret. Both rangefinders controlled the main and secondary batteries. Additionally, the main turret had its own 10,5m rangefinder providing its complete autonomy in case of losing the contact with the fire

A catapult mounted on the turret C of the battleship *Scharnhorst*.

control post. All the data was transmitted to the fire control station located under the armoured deck in the XIV compartment and connected to the main command post via a special communication shaft. When *Gneisenau* was in service, in particular, after the Operation *Berlin*, her turret 'A' was constantly flooded by splashing waves. Therefore, they removed the rangefinder from it and sealed the remaining holes. Besides, the main and secondary batteries featured a 6m rangefinder placed on the forward fire control post. To direct the anti-aircraft fire, they used four 4m SL-6 rangefinders installed at the command posts in gyro-stabilised domes. The data about a target was sent to one of the rooms of the fire control station from where it was transmitted directly to individual guns. The optical equipment was completed by 1,25m portable base rangefinders correcting aims of the light anti-aircraft weapons. In 1939, *Gneisenau* (in October) and *Scharnhorst* (in February) received FuMO 22 radars. The radar antenna was installed on the armoured rangefinder post atop the fore superstructure. While being stationed in Brest, the units received new radar equipment, FuMO 27 and FuMO 21, in the summer of 1941. At the turn of the same year, both ships got equipped with FuMB 'Timor' and 'Sumatra' antennas that could spot operating enemy radar devices.

Two 14,60m catapults were installed on each battleship upon her commissioning. One was placed on the 8m tower behind the aft superstructure. Although it could rotate full 360°, its ability to launch a seaplane was reduced to ¼ and remained within the range of 80-90°. Another catapult was mounted on the stern turret 'C'. Both ships had hangars for seaplanes. *Gneisenau*'s was small enough and could not fulfill its functions properly. It was completely removed in 1939[3]. *Scharnhorst*'s hangar was big and had a catapult on it so she could carry three Arado Ar 196. To operate seaplanes, they used two lattice boom cranes (on each ship they were different) placed on both sides of the hangar and a boom fixed on the stern turret. In the middle of 1939, Ar 196 A-1 from Embarked Air Squadron 1/196 (German: Bordfliegerstaffel 1/196) were taken aboard; later those were changed to Ar 196 A-3. In February 1940, catapults were dismounted from both vessels' aft turrets. Only in the autumn of 1941, they built a bigger hangar on *Gneisenau* in the former catapult area, which allowed launching aircraft directly from within. An additional seaplane with folded wings was stored in its rear section and an extra slipway was atop the hangar.

---

[3] The battleship was meant to carry 4 seaplanes but due to the insufficient hangar size, she could carry 3 seaplanes in theory. In practice, however, only 2 aircraft could be embarked and placed on the catapult.

Chapter 2. Operation service of the battleships and modernisation

Modernisation of *Scharnhorst*

The remodelling of the vessel at the Kriegsmarinewerft shipyard in Wilhelmshaven covered the period of June-August 1939. They changed her clipper bow and the layout of hawse pipes, installed a funnel cap for better discharge of flue gases, extended her hangar and put a catapult on its new roof. Before making similar changes to *Gneisenau*, they removed *Scharnhorst*'s radio topmast located behind the funnel cap and mounted a new one behind the hangar, on which reflector platforms were located. Another little refit took place in December 1939. Atop the forward rangefinder, a radar post featuring a FuMO 22 mattress antenna was arranged. In February 1940, they dismounted the catapult from her turret 'C' as well as the stern boom for launching seaplanes. In May 1940, a cable for demagnetising the MES-device was stretched along her sides. In mid-January 1940, while the she was stationed in Kiel, they began to change 20mm MG C/30 guns to a newer model, MG C/38. In the summer of 1941, she received a FuMO 27 radar mounted on the aft rangefinder post. The admiral's bridge was redesigned by shortening each of two existing bridges by half. Considering the experience with the battleship *Bismark*, they put torpedo tubes on *Scharnhorst*'s decks, which was meant

Crew gathering aboard the *Admiral Scher*. In the background, you can see the battleship *Scharnhorst*.

A photo of the bow of *Scharnhorst* moored to the Wilhelmshaven wharf, taken during the commissioning ceremony on January 9, 1939. An interesting fact is the battleship's coat of arms mounted on the stem: the ship did not have it during the ceremony launching and further equipping. As the photos of the battleship taken between the launching and commissioning show, she only had a painted coat of arms; just before the commissioning, the actual coat of arms was mounted on her hull.

The commissioning ceremony for the battleship *Scharnhorst* took place on January 7, 1939 at Wilhelmshaven base. The command of the ship was taken over by Commander Otto Ciliax – he is actually saluting, standing on a special stand placed on the catapult on the turret C. The photographer caught the moment of hoisting the Kriegsmarine flag onto the stern flagship.

Photo from the bow of *Scharnhorst* moored to a buoy at the roadstead of Heikendorf in Kiel.

The same shot of *Scharnhorst* taken a few seconds later, which is clearly visible in the movements of the people in the bow. The photo also shows a motorboat and a piece of the background behind the ship's stern.

to be 'useful' in sea battles. Torpedo tubes as well as two sets of Flakvierling guns were put on both sides of the hangar. As the British systematically attacked Brest, it was needed to increase the number of the anti-aircraft weapons. One Flakvierling gun was installed on the funnel platform, another one on the turret 'Bruno' and two more were placed on the 150mm twin-gun turrets on the bow; 10 individual 20mm guns C/38 were located in different parts of the ship. One of the last changes was made in February 1942 on her mother waters, while she was stationed at Deutsche Werke in Kiel. The round-shaped radar room on the forward rangefinder was rebuilt into a rectangular-shaped one and FuMO 27 and FuMB 4 'Sumatra' antennas were

installed on it. Furthermore, the rangefinder located inside the turret 'Anton' was removed. Later, in March-April 1942, the admiral's bridge was extended.

Scharnhorst's service history

The ceremonial commissioning of *Scharnhorst* took place on January 7, 1939 and Otto Ciliax became her first commander. During half of the year, he was conducting intensive maritime trials and exercises on the Baltic Sea. After that, the battleship was sent to the shipyard for fitting-out. In July-August 1939, they changed the type of her stem by mounting 'Atlantic

Admiral Raeder aboard paying a visit. Next to the main battery turrets, there are rubber tracks to prevent damage to the deck by cases falling out of the gun turrets.

The battleship *Scharnhorst* photographed en route to the Kaiser Wilhelm Canal.

The main battery turrets firing.

The main battery turrets firing.

The U 47 passing by the *Scharnhorst* after a successful raid to Scapa Flow.

Lifting a seaplane aboard the *Scharnhorst* during the operation code-named Berlin.

bows' to prevent flooding of the bridges by splashing waves. After her stem shape had been considerably sharpened and a small bulbous bow reducing that minor flaw had been added, the battleship became able to fire the main bow turrets without any difficulties. The outbreak of the World War II caught *Scharnhorst* in Brunsbüttel, where British bombers unsuccessfully tried to attack her on September 4, 1939. Four days

The battleship *Scharnhorst* photographed in the winter of 1939/1940.

The battleship *Scharnhorst* photographed in the winter of 1939/1940.

The stern turret of the main battery of *Scharnhorst*.

The battleship *Scharnhorst* photographed in the winter of 1939/1940 during a voyage to the Baltic Sea.

later, together with *Gneisenau*, they sailed through the Kiel Canal to the Baltic Sea, where she was shooting at the target ship *Hessen*. Getting ready for the first joint mission, the battleships took seaplanes aboard and was sent to Wilhelmshaven on November 8. On November 21, 1939, she sailed for the operation together with the cruisers *Köln* and *Leipzig* and her sister *Gneisenau*. Their task was to destroy the British forces patrolling the passage between the Faroe Islands and Iceland. In that raid

attack under the command of vice admiral Marschall, *Scharnhorst* along with *Gneisenau*, which joined her later, sank the British auxiliary armed merchant cruiser HMS *Rawalpindi*. The further trip was interrupted due to the damages *Gneisenau* received in the storm – there were cracks in her hull through which a lot of water leaked inside and that was quite dangerous so both units had to return to Germany on November 27. *Scharnhorst* was moored at the Wilhelmshaven base where they removed

Bow turrets of *Scharnhorst's* main battery.

The battlecruiser H.M.S. *Renown* which the battleships *Gneisenau* and *Scharnhorst* encountered during the operation code-named *Wesserübung*.

During an artillery duel with *Renown*, *Gneisenau* was damaged, which prompted the commander of the crew to interrupt the task and direct the ships towards Germany.

The crew of *Scharnhorst* in combat positions during the operation code-named Juno. It was carried out jointly with the Luftwaffe units, hence, for quick and unmistakable identification by their own aviation, the roofs of the main and secondary battery gun turrets were painted red. In the foreground, we can see the roof and slants of the 150mm gun turret painted in this way. The photo was probably taken on June 8, 1940.

The British aircraft carrier *Glorious* sunk with the escort destroyers by the German battleships *Gneisenau* and *Scharnhorst* during the operation code-named *Juno*.

Firing at the British aircraft carrier *Glorious* from the main battery of the German battleship during the operation code-named *Juno*. A still from a film frame.

minor defects her main turret 'Anton' received. They also installed a FuMO 22 radar on her in December 1939. In mid-January, both battleships went to the Baltic Sea to the measured mile at Neukrug to exercise in firing. After that, she went back to Kiel yet the return trip was difficult due to the thick ice.

Her next operation was *Nordmark*. In February 1940, along with *Gneisenau*, the heavy cruiser *Admiral Hipper* and shield destroyers, *Scharnhorst* was sent to attack British convoys floating between Bergen and Great Britain. Since that operation did not have the desired effect as none of the ships were sunk, German vessels returned to Wilhelmshaven. Two months later, she participated in the invasions of Denmark and Norway – in the Operation *Weserübung*. *Scharnhorst* and *Gneisenau* belonged to the Group 1 that had to transfer German soldiers to Narvik. It did not go without a fight with the British line cruiser HMS *Renown*. On account of damages received by *Gneisenau*, the fleet commander decided to abort the mission and go back to Germany. In the evening of April 12, the fleet safely reached the Wilhelmshaven base. Upon their return, *Scharnhorst* and *Gneisenau* started getting ready for their next operation, *Juno*. During it, the German ships encountered

Along the route of both battleships, there were cases of encounters between neutral units, as it can be seen in the attached photo.

To search for commercial ships and potential enemies, deck seaplanes were used. The photo shows the moment of attaching one of them when it is returning from the patrol.

the British aircraft carrier *Glorious* only escorted by two destroyers. In that short and unequal fight, all the British vessels got sunk yet then HMS *Acasta* came and shoot a torpedo at *Scharnhorst* and struck her near the turret 'C'. Though she had initially been sent to the Trondheim base, the battleship rushed to the Deutsche Werke shipyard in Kiel where necessary repairs were being done till mid-December 1940.

The biggest combat operation in the entire career of *Scharnhorst* was *Berlin*. The first attempt took place on December 28, 1940 yet *Gneisenau* got damaged in the storm and the ships had to turn back. The second one was on January 22, 1941 and turned out to be beneficios as the German battleships crossed the Danish straits and on 3 February and reached South Greenland. *Scharnhorst's* primary target was Convoy HX

106 but she left it in piece when the battleship HMS *Ramillies* was spotted. On March 7-9, the German battleships attacked Convoy SL-67 yet were stopped by the battleship HMS *Malaya* approaching. The operation ended on March 22, 1941 and the ships sailed to Brest. Since March 30, 1941, the Allies were systematically bombarding the local French base, where both ships were stationed, in an attempt to put those out of action. In early April, they conducted a series of harsh air raids on dry docks. Unfortunately, though no bomb hit the battlecruisers, *Gneisenau* was torpedoed. Admiral Lütjens, who visited the battleships on April 14, confirmed that it would take 4 months to mend her engine. Meanwhile, *Scharnhorst* needed to be repaired too and did not participate in any operations until the end of June. In a short while, the heavy cruiser *Prinz*

The second favourite activity of sailors (apart from cleaning the deck) was frequent bathing of the crew on board during voyages on warm waters or in the tropics.

The *Scharnhorst's* mast displaying sunken merchant ships, photographed after arrival in Brest.

Eugen joined *Scharnhorst* and *Gneisenau*. Gathering three heavy battlecruisers in one port was inconvenient and increased the risk of air bombardments, therefore, they decided to transfer *Scharnhorst* to La Pallice on July 23, 1941. Changing of the port delayed the attack on the battleship just for one day as a squadron of 12 Halifax planes successfully bombarded her on July 24. She was hit five times. As her hull was damaged, she inclined 8° to the starboard side and took up to 3,000 t of water inside. Counter-ballasting reduced that heeling to 3° and then to 1°. In that British strike, two crew members were killed and 15 got wounded. Temporarily mended, the ship had to get back to Brest because there were necessary facilities and dry docks. She reached the base in August and stayed there until the end of the year. During the following months, the unit was being repaired and remodelled. In particular, torpedo tubes and additional sets of anti-aircraft Flakvierling guns were installed on her.

At the beginning of 1942, they decided to relocate the whole group to Germany. Due to the short distance from British airports, the German units stationed in Brest were prone to regular bombardments in which they might be severely damaged and, consequently, lose

their fighting abilities. The only solution was sending them to Germany and then to the Baltic Sea. On February 11-13, *Scharnhorst*, *Gneisenau* and *Prinz Eugen* fled through the English Channel to Germany right under the nose of the British. That operation received the kryptonim *Cerberus*. During that passage, *Scharnhorst* hit two mines and was seriously damaged but safely reached the base in Wilhelmshaven. Her repairs lasted till the end of 1942, after which she left the Deutsche Werke shipyard in Kiel and sailed to the Baltic Sea for sea trials there. At the beginning of January, within the Operation *Fronttheater*, she was intended to go from Gotenhafen (modern Gdynia, Poland) to Norway but had to turn back under the threat of being captured by the British forces. The second try was made at the end of January as part of the Operation *Domino* but it failed just like the first one. Only the Operation *Paderborn* ended successfully and, together with *Prinz Eugen*, the battleship entered the fjord near Bergen on March 9, 1943. A few days later, *Scharnhorst* was sent to Altafjord where she stayed till the end of the year. In April, a few serious explosions happened on the ship so she was unable to participate in combat for some time. In September 1943, along with the battleship *Tirpitz*,

Both battleships covered with camouflage nets and tarpaulins, photographed at the docks of Brest in December 1941.

she took part in the Operation *Sizilien*. When *Tirpitz* was disabled, *Scharnhorst* became the most powerful *Kriegsmarine* ship in the North.

Operation *Ostfront* – the sinking of *Scharnhorst*

On December 19, 1943, admiral Dönitz informed Hitler that *Scharnhorst* escorted by the 4th destroyer flotilla was going to attack the next convoy sailing across the Barents Sea. The British Convoy JW 55B departed from Loch Ewe on December 20, 1943. In the meantime, British admiral Fraser, using the information provided by a Norwegian agent, ordered to increase its escort in order to set a trap for the German battleship in case she attacked the convoy. When the latter was spotted, the German

The battleship *Scharnhorst* on Norwegian waters in 1943.

command approved the Operation *Ostfront*. The group comprised of the battleship and destroyers escorting her, led by rear admiral Erich Bey, moved out from Kåfjord to intercept the convoy. The vigilant British received the data from Ultra about the German fleet departing. In the early morning of December 26, 1943, *Scharnhorst* was spotted by the radars of the British cruisers *Norfolk* and *Belfast*. During the first phase of the operation, she was fighting with *Belfast*, *Norfolk* and *Sheffield* that transmitted the data about her course to the battleship *Duke of York*. In this combat, *Scharnhorst*'s radar was struck. Meanwhile, the weather worsened and enlarged the distance between the adversaries. The first phase ended with both attackers stopping the fire. Then the British destroyers that had split up with the Convoy RA 55A escort and joined the cruisers took their action. The second fight was between the British cruisers now supported by the destroyers from the 36th squadron and *Scharnhorst*. On both sides, equally the German battleship and *Norfolk* and *Sheffield* were hit several times. At around 12:50, *Scharnhorst* was moving 138° south trying to sail away to Norway. Nearly 1,5 hours later, admiral Bey commanded captain Johannesson, the commander of the 4th destroyer flotilla, to retreat and go towards Altafjord. Rear admiral did not realise he was approaching the trap set for him. On the other hand, admiral Fraser present on *Duke of York*'s deck concluded that the first contact with the enemy would happen at 17:55 considering *Scharnhorst*'s course and speed. The trap was being locked. *Duke of York* was moving slowly towards the German battleship with all her main weapons ready. At around 16:47, when the distance between the ships

The British battleship Duke of York contributed to the sinking of *Scharnhorst* on the waters of the Barents Sea.

Scharnhorst together with *Tirpitz* made a dangerous couple beyond the Arctic Circle, yet until the latter was eliminated by miniature submarines for a few months. *Scharnhorst* was left alone from the Kriegsmarine heavy ships to fight British convoys.

shortened to 17,500 m, admiral Fraser commanded *Belfast* to fire flares. An unequal fight started between two groups of the British battleships and *Scharnhorst*. As her engine was damaged, the ship's fate was foreseen. She lost the speed advantage and was unable to move away from her adversary. Unable to use her radar and speed, left without any protection from her escort, alone, she was pierced by torpedoes fired by the destroyers *Scorpion* (8 torpedoes from 2,000 m) and *Stord* (8 torpedoes from 1,800 m). One torpedo from *Scorpion* and another three from *Savage* pierced *Scharnhorst*'s right side. Heavily damaged and quickly losing her speed, she got attacked by other British vessels. In order to avoid damaging their own ships, the British stopped firing their main weapons, which enabled them to fire torpedoes from the safe distance. HMS *Belfast* was the first that fired at the unprotected German battle-ship, then HMS *Jamaica* along with the destroyers from the 36th squadron also attacked her4. *Scharnhorst* sank on

December 26, 1943, at around 19:45 as the consequence of the powerful explosion of her bow turrets along with the majority of her crew, only 36 seafarers were saved.

Bibliography

Siegfried Breyer „Schlachtschiffe un Schlachtkreuzer 1921 – 1997. Internationaler Schlachtschiffbau". Bernard & Graefe Verlag. Bonn 2002.

Akta „Gneisenau". Służby techniki i zaopatrzenia DMW. Sygnatura akt 979/2 and 3 „Gneisenau".

Admiral Lütjens Kriegstagebücher (March – April 1941).

Siegfried Breyer „Marine-Arsenal Highlight 2 - Schlachtschiff Gneisenau". Podzun-Pallas -Verlag 2000.

Siegfried Breyer „Marine-Arsenal 3 - Schlachtschiff Gneisenau". Podzun-Pallas -Verlag 1987.

Siegfried Breyer „Marine-Arsenal 32 - Dickschiffe Gneisenau". Podzun-Pallas-Verlag 1995.

Siegfried Breyer „Marine-Arsenal 35 - Dickschiffe Gneisenau". Podzun-Pallas-Verlag 1996.

German Naval Camouflage volume two 1942 – 1945 Eric Leon & John Asmussen.

---

[4]   55 torpedoes were fired at *Scharnhorst* and 11 of them probably pierced her. Furthermore, up to 2,000 shells were shot at her: 446 shells of the calibre 356 mm (14 in) by HMS *Duke of York*, 161 shells of 203 mm (8 in) by HMS *Norfolk*, 874 shells of 152 mm (6 in) by HMS *Jamaica*, HMS *Sheffield* and *Belfast*, 686 shells of 133 mm (5,2 in) by HMS *Duke of York* and 126 shells 120 mm (4,7 in) by the destroyers.

Chapter 3. Photo gallery – „Scharnhorst"

Gerhard Johann David von Scharnhorst

Gerhard Johann David Waitz von Scharnhorst was born on November 12, 1755 in Bordenau upon the Leine near Hanover and spent his early years there. At the age of 17 he entered the military school of Count Wilhelm zu Schaumburg-Lippe at the Wilhelmstein fortress where perfect officers for the small army of the former Principality of Hanover were trained. After he had completed his course at the military academy, Scharnhorst served in the Hanover army since 1778. He transferred to the artillery in 1783. In the course of the following years, he continued comprehending the science of war and simultaneously started to publish his works on it. His first campaign took place in 1793 in Holland. A year later, he participated in the defence of Menen. In a short while after that, Scharnhorst was made major. In 1795, after the Piece of Basel, he returned to Hanover. Being already a known officer, he was offered service in several countries. In 1801, as lieutenant colonel, he joined the service of the King of Prussia and the Military Academy in Berlin employed him as an instructor. Scharnhorst proved himself as a great lecturer and military theorist. During the war with France in 1806, he became the head of the General Staff of Duke of Brunswick. He also fought in the battles of Jena and Auerstedt, where he got slightly injured. Along with Blücher, he was captured after the capitulation of Ratekau and later was exchanged for Napoleon's officers. He played a prominent role in leading the Prussian corps of L'Estocq along with the Russians. For that campaign, he was rewarded with the Pour le Mérite.

In 1806, Scharnhorst got involved in working on modernisation of the Prussian army. Soon after the Peace of Tilsit, he was risen to major general and became the head of the Commission for the Reorganization of the Army aimed at creating a renewed national army. Because of the pressure exerted by France and the loss in the war with Napoleon, the reforms suggested were only implemented partially. Two years later, he became the Minister of War and was named Chief of Staff in 1810. His further military career was closely connected with the existing political situation. In 1811-1812, Prussia was forced to form the alliance with Napoleon against Russia. Disappointed, Scharnhorst left Berlin and retired. However, his leave did not last long as during the retreat of the allied army from Moscow, the King of Prussia made him Chief of Staff to Blücher. In the battle at Lützen that took place on May 2, 1813, Scharnhorst was wounded on his foot. That wound and the lack of appropriate medical treatment led to his death on June 28, 1813 in Prague.

The battleship *Scharnhorst* was photographed immediately after she had been put into service. It is worth paying attention to the second pair of the SL-6 rangefinders, on which three-axis stabilization was tested. The ship has a mast on its funnel and a straight stem.

The launch of the battleship D, *Ersatz Elsaß*, at the Kriegsmarine Werft shipyard in Wilhelmshaven took place on October 3, 1936. The godmother of the ship was the widow of Commander Felix Schultz, the commander of the armoured cruiser *Scharnhorst*. When the bow stoppers were released, the hull began its first journey from the slipway number 2 towards the harbour basin.

Embarkation of the battleship's crew.

The commissioning ceremony for the battleship *Scharnhorst* took place on January 7, 1939 at Wilhelmshaven base. The command of the ship was taken over by Commander Otto Ciliax – he is actually saluting, standing on a special stand placed on the catapult on the turret C. The photographer caught the moment of hoisting the Kriegsmarine flag onto the stern flagship.

One of the crewmen of *Scharnhorst* poses for a photo on the turret A.

On April 1, 1939, the Chancellor of the Third Reich, A. Hitler, visited *Scharnhorst*.

Scharnhorst dressed overall.

Scharnhorst dressed overall, giving a cannon salute at the roadstead of Kiel on April 20, 1939. The occasion for this event was the birthday of the Chancellor of the Third Reich, Adolf Hitler. For propaganda purposes, the photo of the battleship has been heavily retouched.

Scharnhorst moored to the A 12 buoy at the roadstead of Heinkerdorf. On the bow, we can see air supply hoses for a classic dive for underwater visual inspection of this area of the ship.

After the ship had been incorporated into the Kriegsmarine, she spent the first period continuing sea trials on the waters of the North Sea and the Baltic Sea. Here we see *Scharnhorst* at the mouth of the Jade River in Wilhelmshaven, sailing for another round of sea trials scheduled for the second half of April 1939.

Scharnhorst on the high seas. On September 8, 1939, the battleship sailed to the Baltic Sea, where it conducted artillery firing at the target ship *Hessen*.

The battleship *Scharnhorst* on the waters of Wilhelmshaven in the summer of 1939, right after her reconstruction was finished. It was carried out at the Kriegsmarine Werft shipyard and included, among others: changing her stem to a so-called Atlantic one, changing the funnel cover to a new one and installing a new, three-legged mast behind the aircraft hangar. The reconstruction carried out between June and August 1939 significantly changed the previous silhouette of the battleship. A retouched photo.

A shot of *Scharnhorst* taken a few minutes after the previous photo. A very common practice used in the photos of the battleship was the removal of the military background by the censor – in this case the buildings of Wilhelmshaven. This operation was to make it impossible to determine the place and date when the photo had been taken.

Another shot of *Scharhorst* made after the modernisation of the battleship with a new stem and the mast shifted towards the stern.

On November 8, 1939, during *Scharnhorst's* stay in Kiel, four Ar 196 seaplanes were taken on board of the ship. The photo shows two of them put on the catapults.

Another shot of *Scharnhorst* with the seaplanes on the catapults.

On the catapult, above the hangar roof, the Arado 196 A1 numbered T3+NH is ready for a start. Replacing the previous seaplanes with new ones did not go without problems: by the end of 1939, the Arado aircraft company only produced 20 copies. The first version, the A1, was included in the equipment for the Kriegsmarine units from June 1939.

The Arado (T3 + NH) ready for catapulting. As you can see in the photo, the machine does not yet have the 1/196 Bordfligerstafflel emblem painted, which was a white seahorse on a silver shield surrounded by a black border. Presumably, the plane was assigned to equip *Scharnhorst* as soon as it left the Arado plant.

A watch on the battleship *Scharnhorst*.

The battleship *Scharnhorst* photographed in early December 1939. The fore superstructure is already mounted on top of the platform over a 10.5-metre rangefinder with a FuMO 22 radar antenna.

The foredeck being flooded by rough seas.

Another shot showing the flooding of the foredeck by rough seas. It made it difficult to accurately aim with the help of a rangefinder mounted in the turret Anton.

The foredeck of *Scharnhorst*. It is worth paying attention to the storage bins on the roof of the turret Bruno.

The bow superstructure of *Scharnhorst*.

The battleship *Scharnhorst* on the high seas in December 1939. The photo was taken during successive attempts to catapult the Arado Ar 196 A1 from a new catapult capable of launching aircraft of greater weight. One of them, after being picked up from the water, is being transferred to the battleship's hangar.

Washing the main deck was a typical activity for sailors while the vessel was in port. The photo showing the aft turret of the battleship *Scharnhorst* was taken in November 1939 at the roadstead in Wilhelmshaven.

The battleship *Scharnhorst* photographed in early December 1939 at the Kriegsmarine Werft shipyard in Wilhelmshaven. At the top of thefore superstructure, the FuMO 22 radar antenna is already mounted with a 10.5-metre rangefinder. In the background, you can see *Tirpitz's* hull moored to the shipyard's equipment quay.

The battleship *Scharnhorst* being towed from the Kriegsmarine Werft shipyard after the completion of the December modernisation.

The funnel of the battleship *Scharnhorst* next to the main mast. The photo had been taken before the battleship underwent modernisation.

The battleship *Scharnhorst* moored to the H1 wharf in the Hipper Basin in Wilhelmshaven. In the photo probably taken in early March 1940, we see the training of new machine crew commanders conducted on the quayside. In the background, the battleship catapult is attached to the Lange Heinrich floating crane, which will soon be removed from the turret C.

A shot from the training of the battleship's crew, this time taken amidships – an aeroplane hangar is visible in the centre. Next to the catapult, the Arado Ar 196 seaplane numbered T3+NH is actually being hidden in the hangar.

The main bow battery turrets prepared for calibration firing. This photo was taken after December 1939 as evidenced by the mounted radar antenna.

The battleship *Gneisenau* (in the background) photographed from the *Scharnhorst*'s bridge in December 1939 during the stay of both ships in Wilhelmshaven.

The battleship *Scharnhorst* photographed at the beginning of December 1939 at the Kriegsmarine Werft shipyard in Wilhelmshaven. In the foreground, a group of sailors are standing in front of the turret C.

Cleaning the barrels of the main battery.

Scharnhorst on the way to the Baltic Sea, photographed while crossing the Kaiser Wilhelm Canal.

During the stay of *Scharnhorst* on the Baltic Sea in January 1940, she spent most of her time on calibration shooting with the target ship Hessen.

On the Baltic Sea. A break in calibration shooting.

The battleship *Scharnhorst* photographed on the Baltic Sea during the calibration shooting carried out together with the target ship *Hessen*.

On the Baltic Sea. Seamen from the crew of *Scharnhorst* posing for a commemorative photo. As you can see in the photo, the ship is heavily icy. The mass of ice gave her several dozen additional tonnes, which had to be removed by the crew.

Scharnhorst's icy gun turrets.

Another shot, this time showing the icy barrels of *Scharnhorst's* guns.

Painting of the upper fore superstructure.

One of the battleship's crewmen wearing a winter uniform.

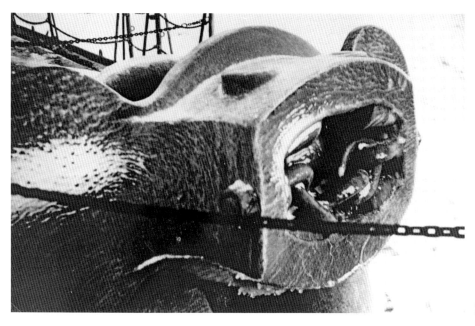

Icy main anchor on the port side.

Seamen from the crew of the battleship photographed on the icebound Bay of Kiel.

Both *Scharnhorst* and *Gneisenau* performed calibration shooting with the target ship Hessen.

Calibration shooting on the Baltic Sea.

Cleaning of the barrels by the staff of the gun turrets carried out in winter conditions.

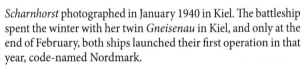

Scharnhorst photographed in January 1940 in Kiel. The battleship spent the winter with her twin *Gneisenau* in Kiel, and only at the end of February, both ships launched their first operation in that year, code-named Nordmark.

During their stay in Kiel, the crew of the battleship spent most of their time free from watches and official duties outside the unit posing for commemorative photos against the backdrop of winter accents.

The battleship trapped in ice. In the foreground, we see the seamen from the ship's crew.

Scharnhorst at the H1-Hipperhafen wharf in Wilhelmshaven, photographed in March 1940 from the deck of the U-50 sailing out. Despite the foggy day, you can easily see the catapult is absent on the battleship's turret C.

A view of the battleship's aircraft hangar. In the foreground, an Arado with folded wings is being hidden in the hangar.

The first seaplane for Scharnhorst placed on a cart and prepared for folding the wings. Soon it will be hidden in the aircraft hangar.

Staff that handled searchlights and guns occupying combat positions on the funnel platform – the alarm mode. In the background, there is the catapult and *Scharnhorst's* mast. The photo as from March 1940.

Scharnhorst photographed in the spring of 1940 at the quay at the sea station in Gotenhafen.

An escort of destroyers and torpedo boats anchored in the vicinity of the battleship.

The battleship *Scharnhorst* anchored at the roadstead in Wilhelmshaven, April 1940. Based on the painting, it can be assumed that the photo was taken before the operation *Waserübung* (April 7-12, 1940).

On the way into Norwegian waters.

The crew in combat positions.

On Norwegian waters.

Operation *Juno*. In the foreground of *Scharnhorst, Gneisenau* is visible.

A photo of *Scharnhorst* (in the foreground) taken from aboard the battleship *Gneisenau* during Operation *Juno*. A salvo of the battleship's bow guns fired towards a British carrier.

Another shot of the salvo from the battleship's bow fired at the British aircraft carrier HMS *Glorious* during the duel on June 8, 1940.

The secondary battery firing at the aircraft carrier HMS *Glorious*.

A salvo of the *Scharnhorst's* bow guns.

A salvo of the *Scharnhorst's* bow guns.

Night shooting by the twin ship, *Gneisenau*.

Both *Scharnhorst* and *Gneisenau* were equipped with the Arado Ar 196 seaplanes. One of them was photographed while flying near the battleship.

Raising the Arado seaplane on board the *Scharnhorst*.

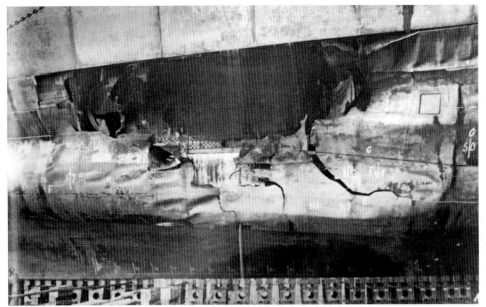

Damage to *Scharnhorst* after she was torpedoed by HMS *Acasta*. It was hastily repaired, and the battleship underwent engine testing on June 18, 1940, which was successful. On June 20, she left Trondheim and sailed towards Kiel, arriving on June 23. The next day she was placed in the drydock C of the Deutsche Werke shipyard. The photo shows damage to the stern part of the battleship.

At the roadsted of Trondheim.

Another shot of the German squad on Norwegian waters.

A photo of *Scharnhorst* (in the foreground) taken from the deck of *Gneisenau*.

The heavy cruiser Admiral *Hipper* (in the foreground) and the battleship *Scharnhorst* photographed during a stop on Norwegian waters during the operation code-named *Juno*.

The moment a seaplane is taking off from the deck of *Gneisenau*.

Operation *Berlin*. A conversation between senior officers.

Operation *Berlin*. The crew of *Scharnhorst* free from a watch, spending their time singing.

Another prey of the German battleship sunk during the operation code-named *Berlin*.

Scharnhorst's prey sinking.

Handling the 10.5cm anti-air-craft guns at the combat positions.

The crew of *Scharnhorst* during an alarm activity.

Operation *Berlin*. It is worth paying attention to the remnants of the beam camouflage preserved amidships *Scharnhorst*.

A photo showing sailors from the ships sunk by *Scharnhorst* leaving the deck of the battleship after mooring in Brest in March 1941.

Scharnhorst moored to the quay in Brest. The photo was taken after the end of Operation *Berlin*, at the end of March 1941. Soon the British intelligence found out about the stay of this ship and *Gneisenau* in port and decided to eliminate both units from service at any cost. The only way to do this was to torpedo or bomb the battleship.

The first raids on the German battleships stationed in Brest began on the last night of March 1941. To make it difficult for the enemy to recognize *Scharnhorst* moored at the quay, she was covered with masking nets. Her armament was also strengthened by placing additional guns on the quay. The photo shows a masked *Scharnhorst* at the Brest waterfront, mid-April 1941.

During her stay in Brest, all possible identification marks were removed: it was feared that those would be handed over to the British by French agents. In the foreground, we see one of the embarked seaplanes with a painted emblem and tactical numbers. The Arado flew from Wilhelmshaven to Brest on June 12, 1941. As it soon turned out, covering the ship with camouflage nets was insufficient and it was decided to additionally cover the upper parts of the superstructures with camouflage.

One of the battleship's seaplanes is flying above the ship. Its task was to perform reconnaissance flights and photograph the battleship. On the basis of a series of aerial photos, it was possible to quickly remove errors in the unit's camouflage.

A gathering of the battleship crew at the stern of the vessel.

Grand Admiral Raeder is speaking to the crew of *Scharnhorst*.

A photo from air reconnaissance of Brest taken in December 1941 shows both battleships in dry docks covered with camouflage nets. On the left, marked as No. 1, is the battleship *Scharnhorst*, No. 2 on the right is the battleship *Gneisenau*.

The crossing of the English Channel in February 1942 by three German heavy ships: *Scharnhorst, Gneisenau* and *Prinz Eugen* was code-named Operation *Cerberus*. The shield destroyer photographed from the deck of the Scharnhorst during the start of the operation.

Operation *Cerberus*. The German squad on their way through the English Channel.

Operation *Cerberus*. A shield is composed of torpedo boats; *Scharnhorst* is visible in the background.

In the photo taken from the deck of the battleship *Gneisenau*, we can see the flagship of the squad, *Scharnhorst*, on board of which was the commander, Vice Admiral Ciliax.

Operation *Cerberus*. An escort of torpedo boats and destroyers shielding the *Scharnhorst* sailing inside.

A photograph taken on February 12, 1942 from the deck of the heavy cruiser *Prinz Eugen* after *Scharnhorst* first hit a mine. British mines were dropped from the Hampdens between February 6 and 11, during the channel mining operation, also Operation *Nectarine*. The commander, Vice Admiral Ciliax, transferred his flag to the destroyer Z 29, assigning the 3rd Torpedo Flotilla to shield the battleship.

During Operation *Cerberus*, the battleship Scharnhorst hit a mine twice and was badly damaged. The photo shows *Scharnhorst* with a slight bow trim, it was probably made from the destroyer Z 29.

Scharnhorst during Operation *Cerberus*.

A still from a film made during Operation *Cerberus*.

Gneisenau visible from the deck of *Scharnhorst*. Operation *Cerberus*.

Gneisenau and *Prinz Eugen* visible from the deck of *Scharnhorst*. Operation *Cerberus*.

Gneisenau and *Prinz Eugen* visible from the deck of *Scharnhorst*. Operation *Cerberus*.

Scharnhorst, *Gneisenau* and *Prinz Eugen* visible from the deck of the shield destroyer.

During Operation *Cerberus*, before midnight, around 10:34 p.m., *Scharnhorst* again hit a mine north of Terschelling. About 1,000 tonnes of water flowed into the hull of the battleship, and turbines and generators were damaged. The battleship was able to reach a speed of 15 knots, but luck did not leave her completely and the following day, around 12:30, she reached Wilhelmshaven base.

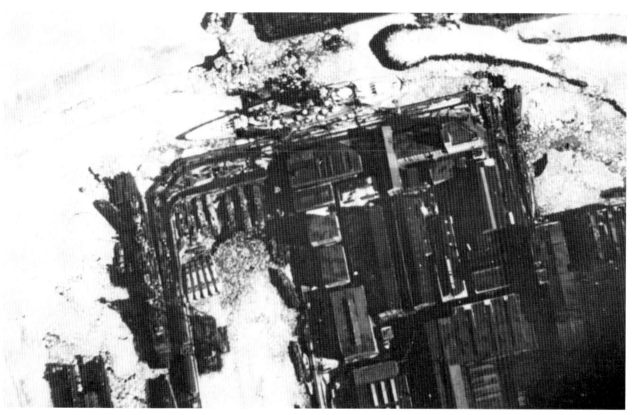

An aerial photo of the Deutsche Werke shipyard in Kiel, taken in March 1942 by British aerial reconnaissance. At the top of the photo, *Scharnhorst* surrounded by ice is moored to the quay, while on the left, we see the cruiser *Nürnberg* tied to the pier.

A board dispalying the shoodowns of planes by the armament.

Sailors serving in the kitchen peeling cabbage.

The battleship *Scharnhorst* in Bogen Bay near Narvik, March 9 or 10, 1943. The operation of ferrying the battleship into Norwegian waters was code-named Paderborn and was successful. On the right side of the photo, you can see the destroyer *Erich Steinbrink*.

Scharnhorst photographed on Norwegian waters with *Emden*.

Scharnhorst firing torpedoes.

The battleship *Scharnhorst* photographed from the deck of *Tirpitz* in September 1943.

The battleship *Scharnhorst* on Norwegian waters.

The battleships *Scharnhorst* (left) and *Tirpitz* photographed in September 1943 during the attack on Spitsbergen. This operation under the command of Vice Admiral Kummetz was code-named *Sizilien*. Both German ships destroyed coal installations, port and transhipment facilities on the island with the fire of their main batteries.

The battleship *Scharnhorst* on Norwegian waters, photographed from the deck of the destroyer Z 10.

Sailors rescued from *Scharnhorst*.

Chapter 4. Stereoscopic photos of *Scharnhorst*

Cleaning of the deck by the crew of *Scharnhorst* was routine work on board in port. The photographer captured this process during the stay of the battleship at the roadstead in Wilhelmshaven in May 1940, before the start of the operation code-named *Juno*.

A group of sinalmen exercising on the aft deck of *Scharnhorst*. Ventilation shafts are visible in the background along with one of the bases of the stern mast.

Cleaning of the deck by the crew of the battleship *Scharnhorst*. In this photo, we can see a stripe painted on the ship's bow superstructure. This photo was taken while the battleship was staying at the roadstead in Wilhelmshaven in May 1940, before the start of the operation code-named *Juno*.

Exercises of individual squadrons of sailors on board the battleship *Scharnhorst*; in this case, the photographer captured the moment of training a group of marine sinalmen who are perfecting the transmission of signals in the Morse code using flags. In the background, you can see the gun turret with a calibre of 10.5 cm S.K.C / 33 at 8.8 cm Dopp. LC./31.

Scharnhorst's bow superstructure with individual decks, seen from the right side of the boat deck.

One of the routine activities of seamen during the vessel's stay in port were gymnastic exercises on board the *Scharnhorst*. In the vicinity of the turrets B and C, there were special holders in the deck for attaching gymnastic bars.

Cleaning and washing the bow turrets and main battery guns. For this purpose, the turret A has the barrels of its guns set to the minimum position to facilitate the work of the staff. This photo was taken while the battleship was staying in Wilhelmshaven.

Maintenance and painting of the funnel of the battleship *Scharnhorst* carried out by the crew in April 1940.

The crew exercising in lowering the lifeboat to water.

The bow superstructure of *Scharnhorst* photographed in April 1940 on the waters of Wilhelmshaven. The battleship has characteristic elements for quick identification that allow her native aviation to recognize the ship without errors. These included the national flag painted on the fore and aft decks, and the roofs and slants of the main and secondary battery turrets of a color different from the rest of the ship. In the far right, the battleship Gneisenau is barely visible.

Checking the cleanliness of one of the bow winches. In the background, we can see the main battery turrets of *Scharnhorst* visible from the foredeck. The roofs and slants of the turrets are painted red. The picture was taken on the waters of Wilhelmshaven in April 1940, before the start of Operation *Wasserübung*.

The crew exercising in lowering the lifeboat to water.

A crew gathering on the bow deck of the battleship.

A crew gathering in the stern of the battleship. Behind the seamen, there is a national flag painted as an identification mark for their native aviation.

The battleship *Scharnhorst* anchored at the roadstead of Wilhelmshaven, April 1940. Based on the painting, it can be assumed that the photo was taken before the Operation *Waserübung* started on April 7, 1940.

The crew exercising amidships the battleship *Scharnhorst*.

Handling of the 10.5cm anti-air-craft guns photographed during the inspection on the battleship *Scharnhorst*.

The boat deck on *Scharnhorst* between the superstructure and the ship's funnel. In the foreground, one of the vessel's communication boats is mounted on the joists, with the crane arm visible above it. This photo was taken, like the previous one, during the preparation of the battleship for Operation *Wasserübung*.

Removal of artillery grease from a 105mm cartridge. In the background, we can see a 105mm training gun – it was used by the gun operator for practical training, thanks to which the gun lock was saved and protected from damage.

The main artillery turrets of the battleship *Scharnhorst*.

The slopes of the turret A painted red – easy to recognize even in difficult weather conditions – allowing to unmistakably identify a German battleship, in this case the *Scharnhorst*.

A moment of entertainment at the port. The crew of the battleship *Scharnhorst* are playing cards.

Handling of the 37mm aft gun at the combat position. One of the seamen is wearing sunglasses allowing him to accurately observe the horizon. This photo was taken aboard the battleship *Scharnhorst* during the preparations for Operation *Juno*.

Handling of the engine room service at combat positions.

Painting the starboard crane for lifting seaplanes and communication boats on *Scharnhorst*. Other crane arms were mounted on this battleship and on the twin *Gneisenau*, which allows the unit to be identified.

Sailors free from the watch could play cards on board in their free time.

Preparation of meals by chefs. In the photo, one of the cooks is pouring the sauce onto the previously fried cutlets.

Launching a lifeboat.

The exercises of the battleship's crew in individual squadrons wcrc performed on board of the battleship in good weather.

The ship kitchen. In the foreground, one of the cooks is preparing a meal for the crew.

One of the onboard seaplanes of *Scharnhorst* photographed while flying near the battleship.

The ship office.

Chapter 5. 3D visualization of *Scharnhorst*

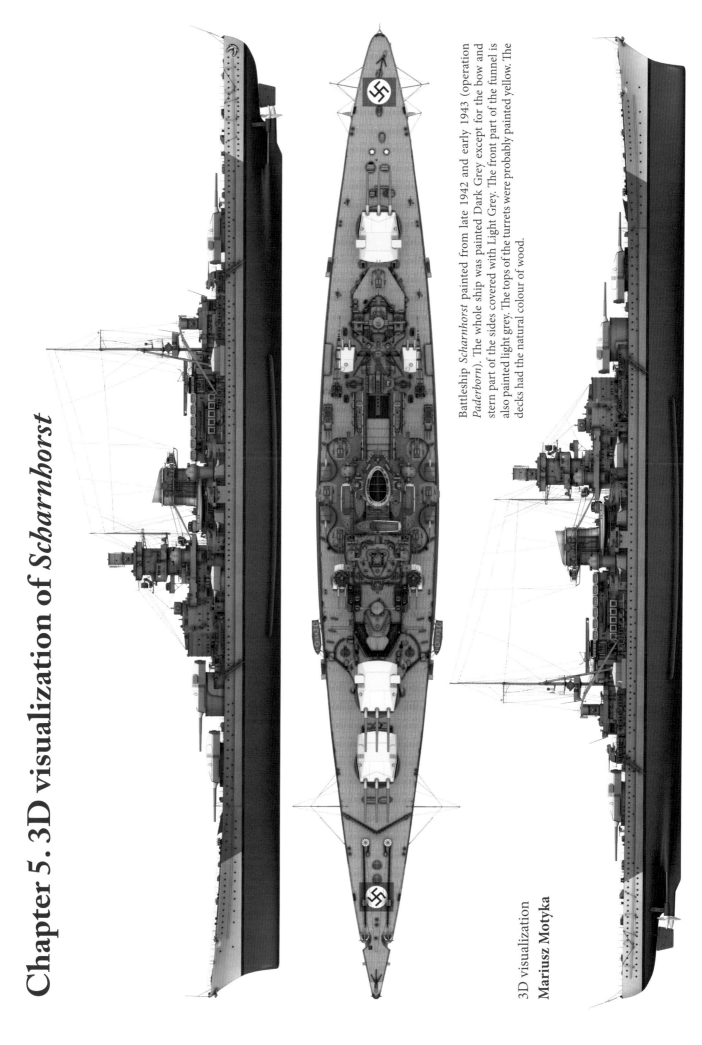

Battleship *Scharnhorst* painted from late 1942 and early 1943 (operation *Paderborn*). The whole ship was painted Dark Grey except for the bow and stern part of the sides covered with Light Grey. The front part of the funnel is also painted light grey. The tops of the turrets were probably painted yellow. The decks had the natural colour of wood.

3D visualization
Mariusz Motyka

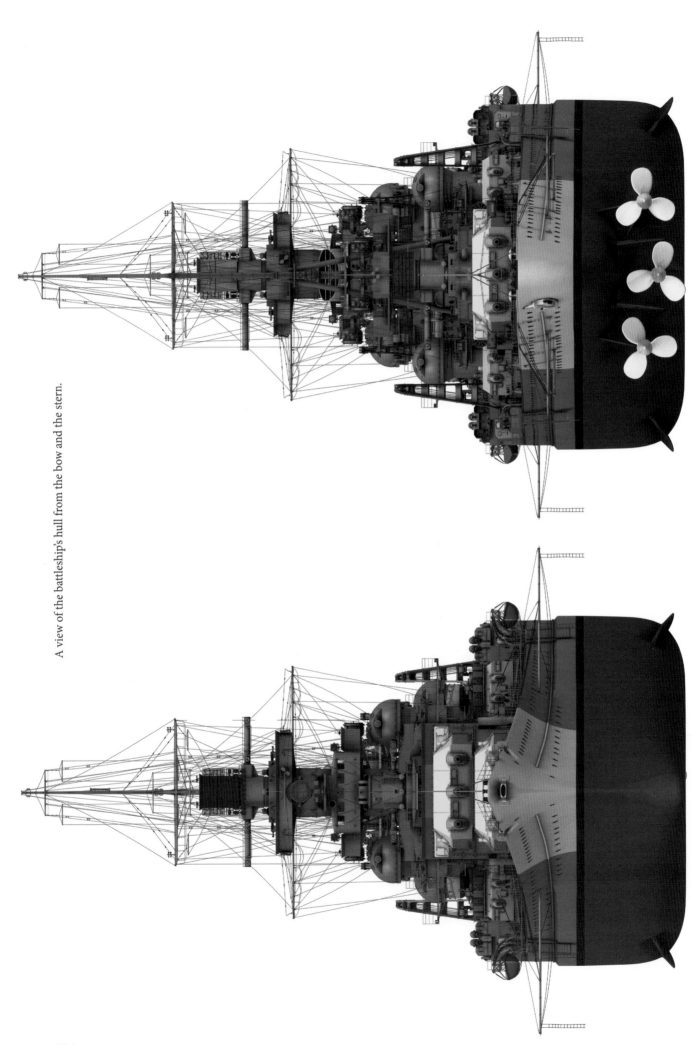

A view of the battleship's hull from the bow and the stern.

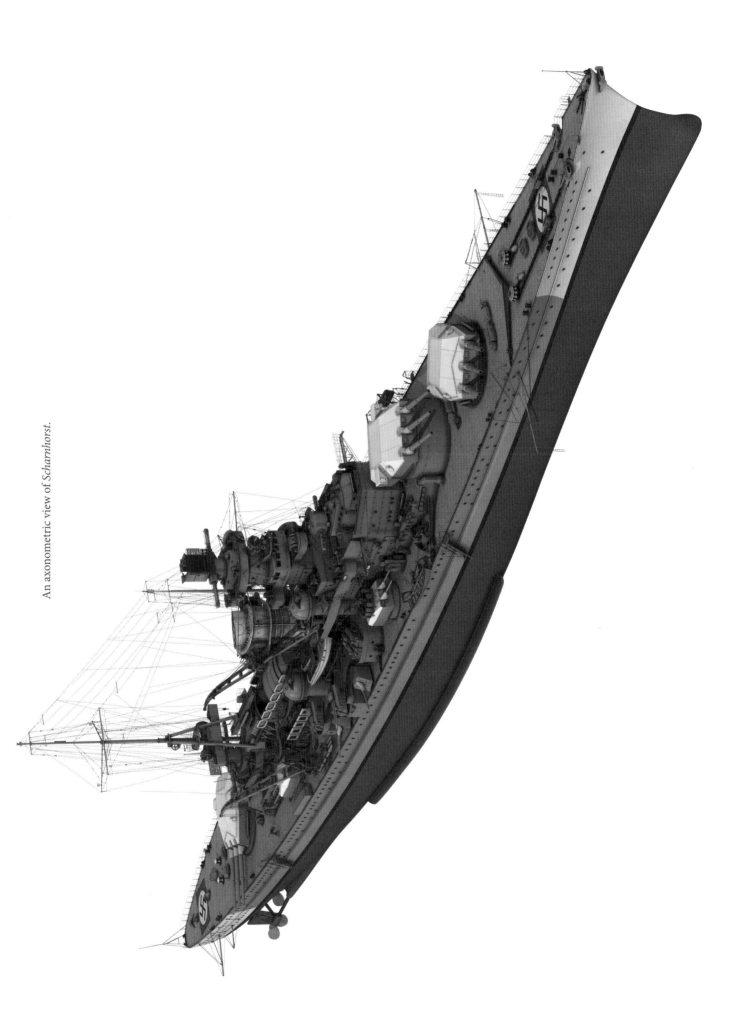

An axonometric view of Scharnhorst.

A view from the top of the bow structure of the superstructure.

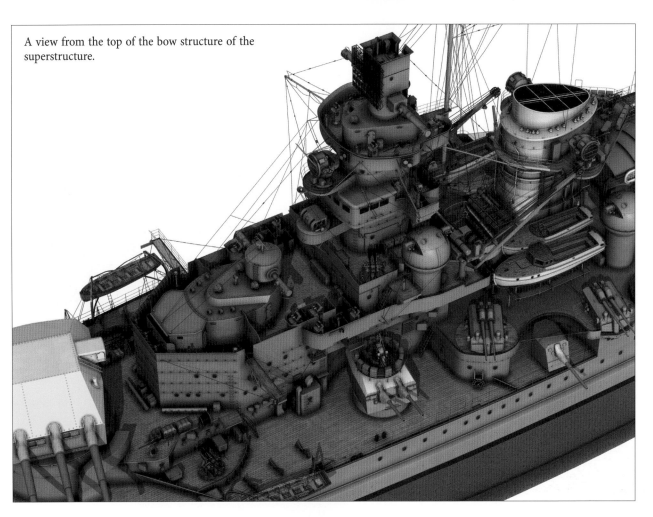

A view of the midship at the height of the funnel on the starboard side showing the arrangement of communication boats and the positions of the cranes serving those. On the left side, you can see the base and the SL-6 fire control station.

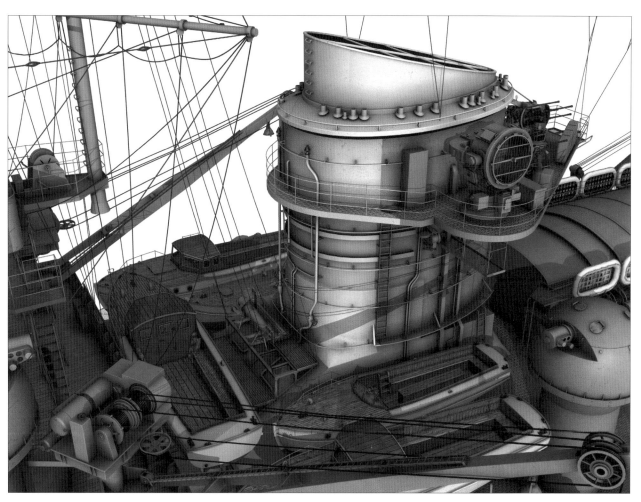

The painting of the main funnel.

The structure of the bow superstructure. The starboard view.

The port side view of the stern part of the battleship. The three-legged aft mast and its rigging are highly visible.

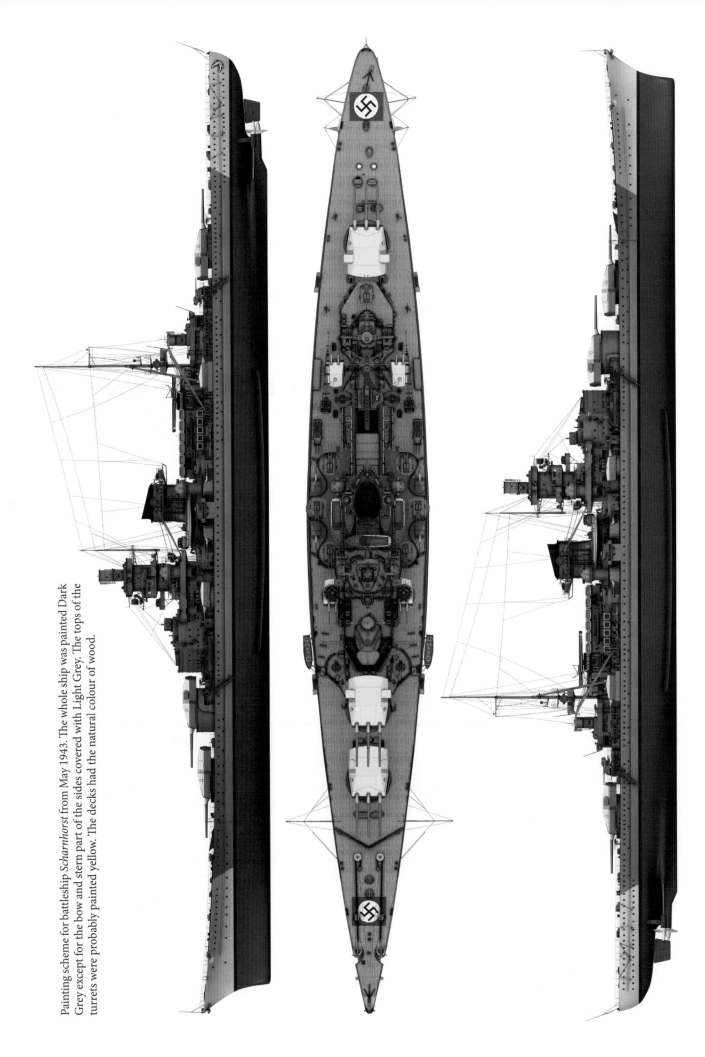

Painting scheme for battleship *Scharnhorst* from May 1943. The whole ship was painted Dark Grey except for the bow and stern part of the sides covered with Light Grey. The tops of the turrets were probably painted yellow. The decks had the natural colour of wood.

130

The battleship in May 1943.
A view of the hull symmetry from the bow and the stern.

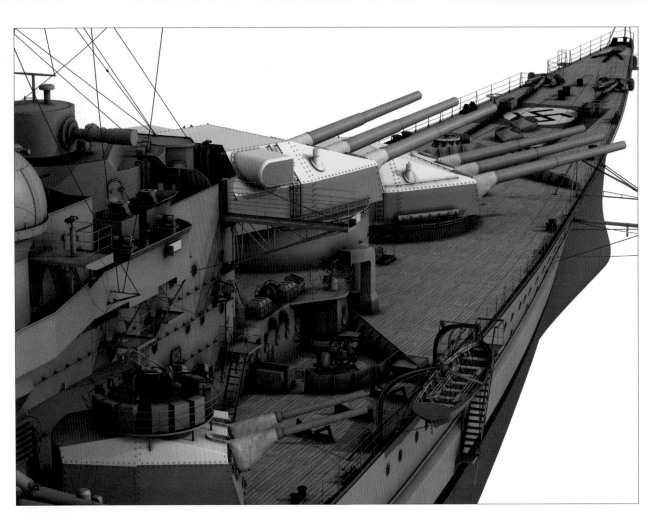

The bow turrets of the main battery as seen from the stern. It is worth paying attention to the recognition markings for the Luftwaffe, i.e. the roofs and slants of the turrets and the national flag painted on the deck.

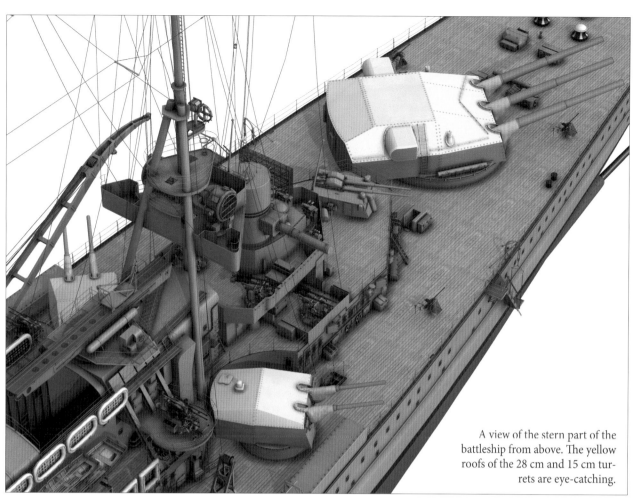

A view of the stern part of the battleship from above. The yellow roofs of the 28 cm and 15 cm turrets are eye-catching.

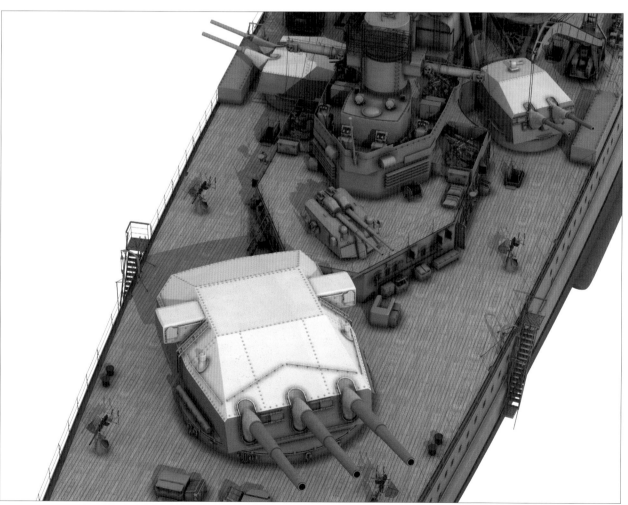

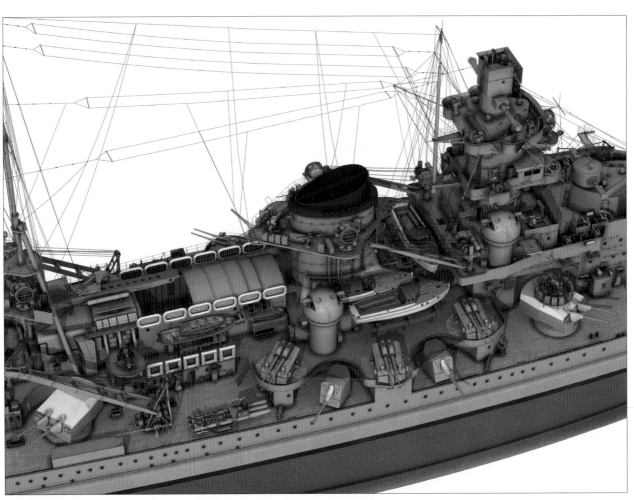

An axonometric view of the midship of the battleship. The starboard armament is clearly visible.

A view from the port side showing the 28 cm gun turrets "A" and "B" and the superstructure in May 1943.

Painting scheme for battleship Scharnhorst from September 1943. Five colours were used for painting the ship: two basic colours of Dunkelgrau, white and black, and light blue-grey and medium blue-grey. The decks had the natural colour of wood.

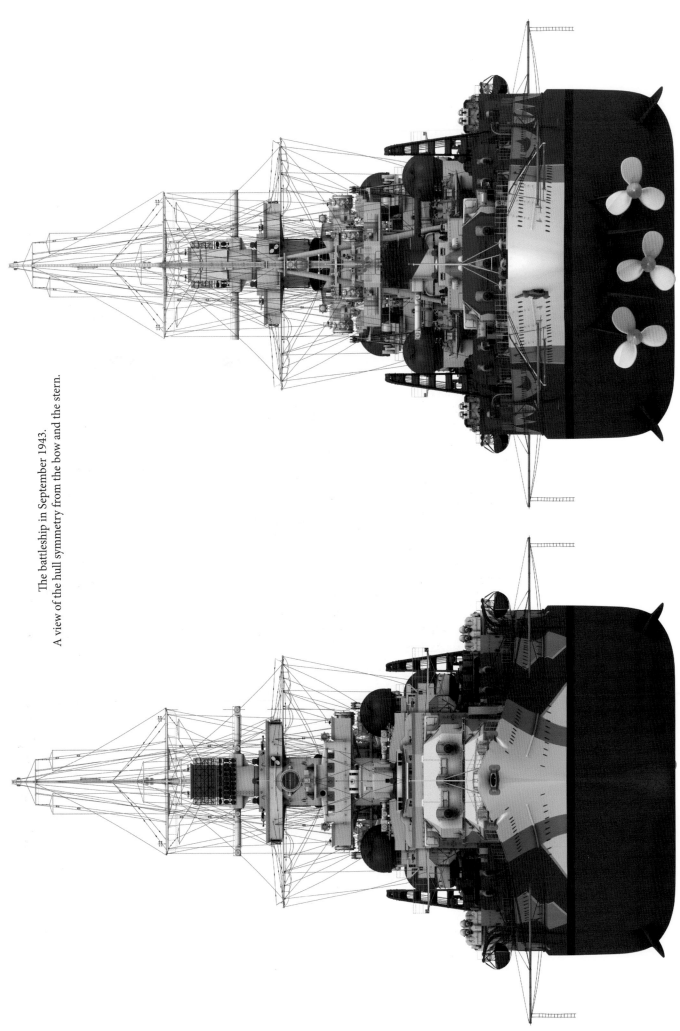

The battleship in September 1943.
A view of the hull symmetry from the bow and the stern.

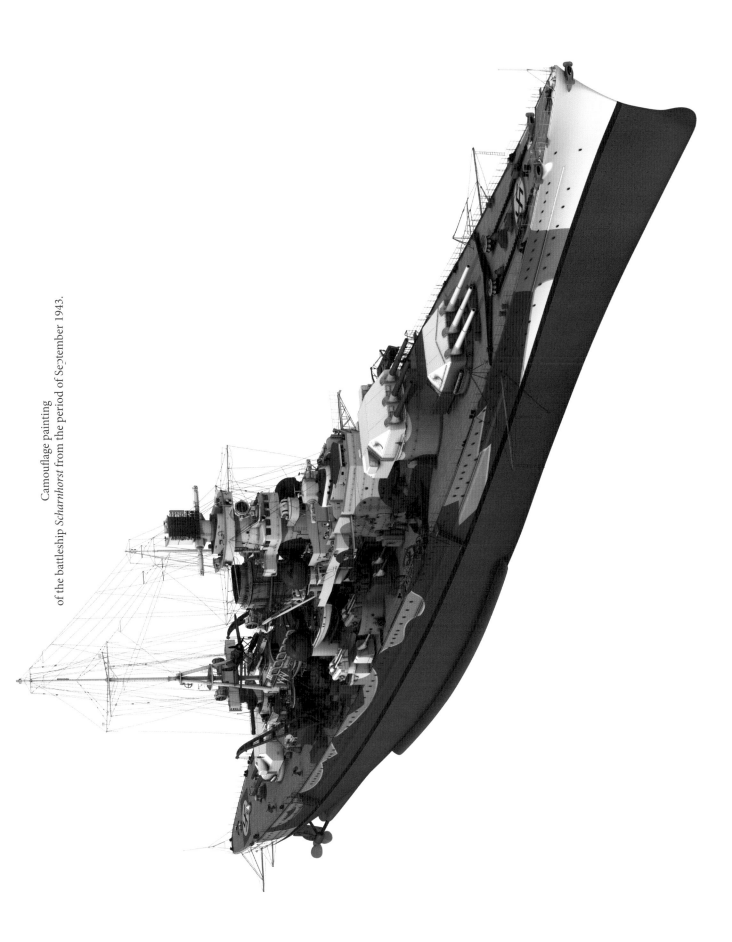

Camouflage painting
of the battleship *Scharnhorst* from the period of September 1943.

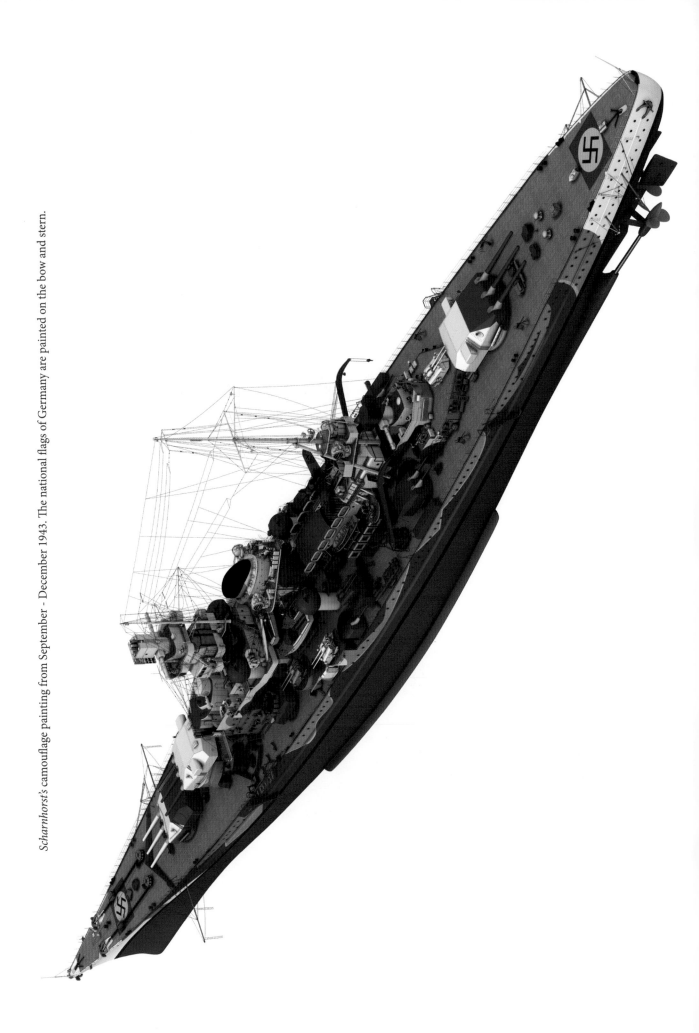

Scharnhorst's camouflage painting from September - December 1943. The national flags of Germany are painted on the bow and stern.

Details of *Scharnhorst*'s camouflage painting as of September - September 1943.

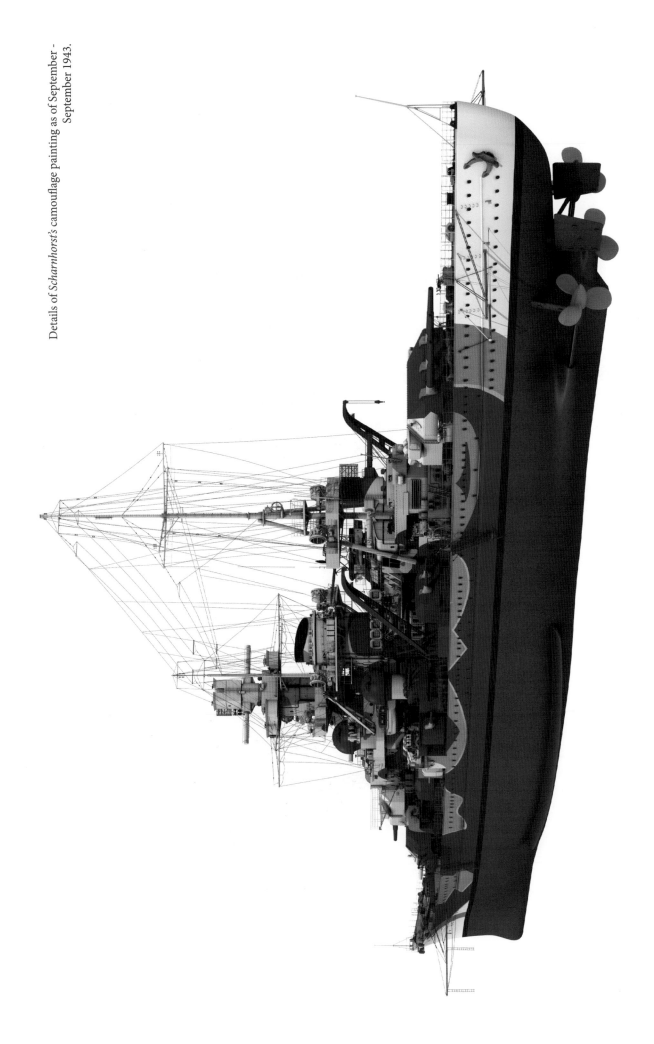

Details of *Scharnhorst's* camouflage painting as of September - September 1943.

A view from the stern of the battleship's port side. The foreground features the seaplane crane and the three-legged aft mast. The hangar and the funnel are visible in the background.

The camouflage layout amidships the Scharnhorst. View of part of the funnel and the bow superstructure from the stern. Eye-cathcing is the construction of the supports of the funnel platform on which they installed. 20 mm AA guns and two reflectors with a mirror diameter of 1.6 metres.

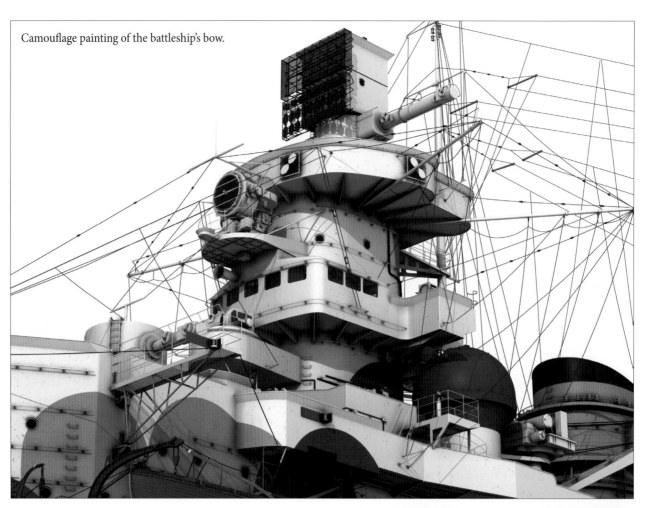
Camouflage painting of the battleship's bow.

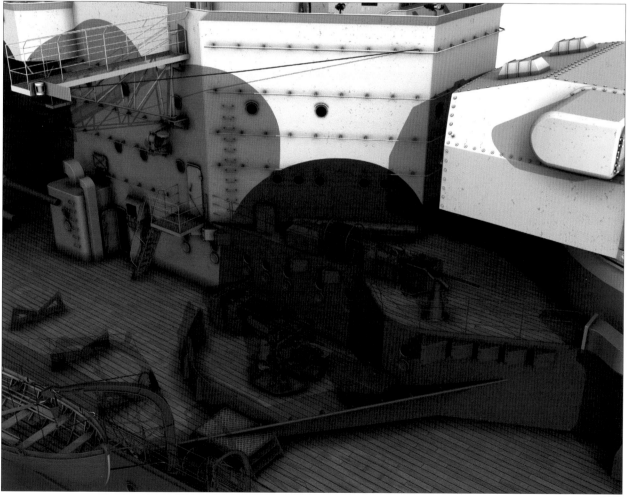

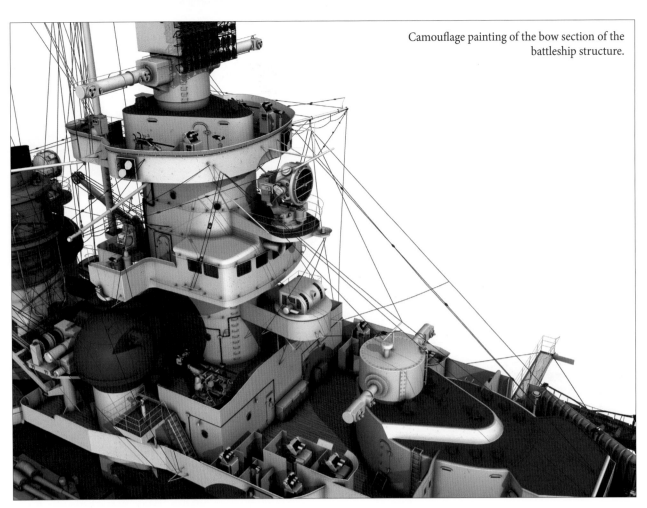

Camouflage painting of the bow section of the battleship structure.

Details of the equipment of the fore part of the battleship
structure and the distribution of camouflage spots.

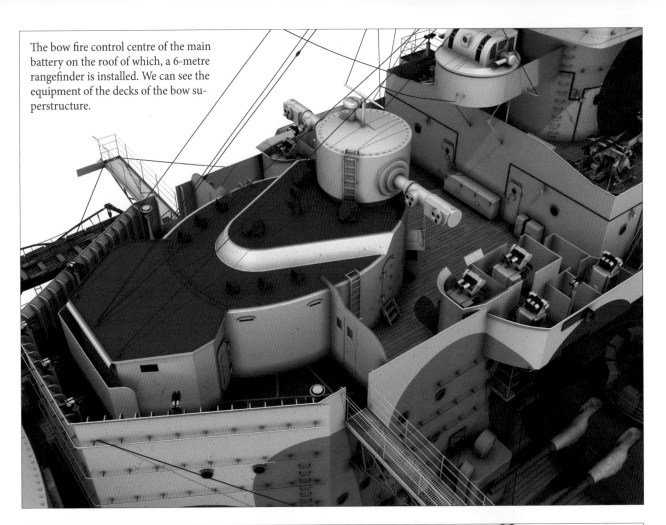

The bow fire control centre of the main battery on the roof of which, a 6-metre rangefinder is installed. We can see the equipment of the decks of the bow superstructure.

The structure of the aft superstructure with full equipment seen from the stern.

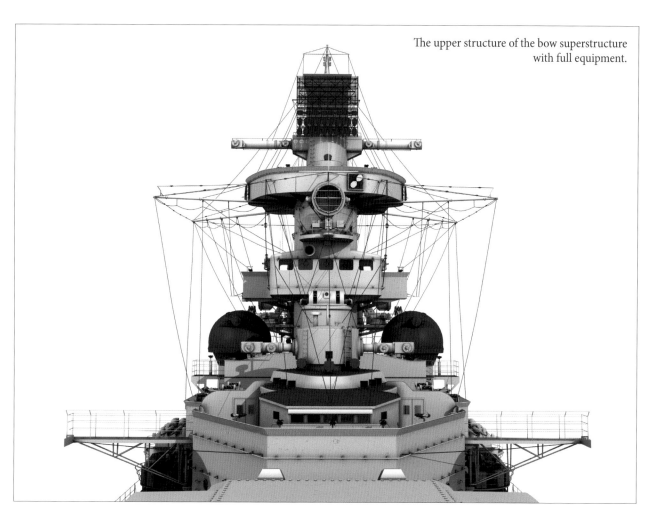

A view of the bow 15 cm gun turret. On the roof of the turret, you can see the 20 mm C 35 FlakVierlig installed in 1942.

The midship from the port side. The base of the SL-6 mount is clearly visible, allowing you to quickly distinguish both battleships from each other. On *Scharnhorst* it was truncated and on *Gneisenau* it was semicircular.

A view from the bow on the starboard side of the entire bow superstructure.

A front view of the 150 mm gun turret on the starboard side, the bow part.

The funnel in all its glory seen from above with a perfectly presented platform for spotlights and 20 mm AA guns with their ammunition boxes.

A view of the midship from the port side. In the foreground, we can see the funnel with its equipment.

A top view of the funnel and a fragment of the hangar cover to which life rafts were attached on both sides in 1943.

The midship of the battleship. Artillery outfitting details.

Top view from the port side amidships of the battleship. The positions of 10.5 cm AA guns and 15 cm secondary battery are highly visible.

A view of the battleship's hangar. The roof cover segments are clearly visible.

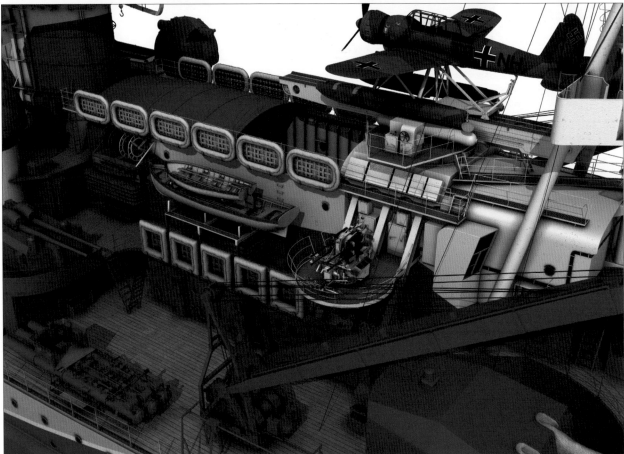

Top view of the battleship's aircraft hangar. Above you can see the Arado 196 plane placed on a catapult. Below the catapult were the positions of the quadruple 20mm AA cannons.

The starboard side view of the hangar. On both sides of the hangar, two 8-meter long cutters were placed on the joists, and two 5-metre yawls were put on those.

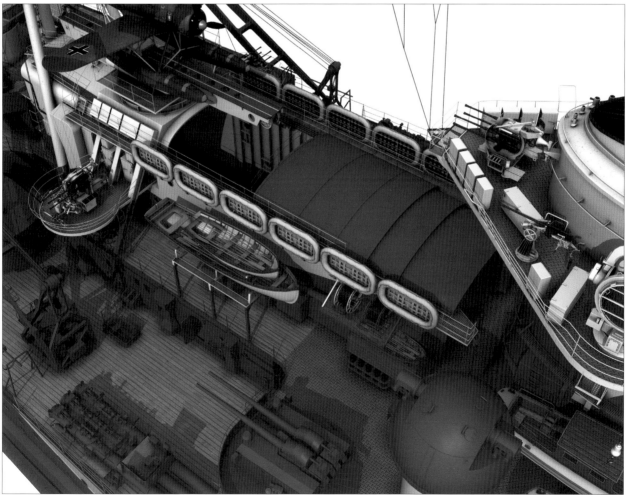

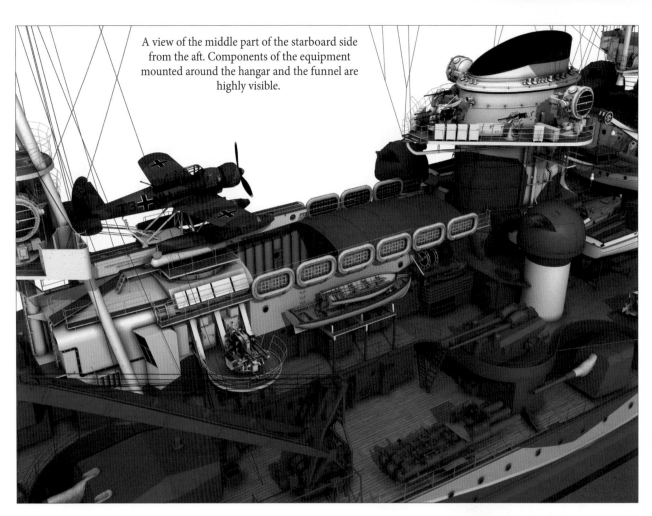

A view of the middle part of the starboard side from the aft. Components of the equipment mounted around the hangar and the funnel are highly visible.

A view of the aft superstructure from the port side and the position of 37 mm AA guns of the plot located on it.

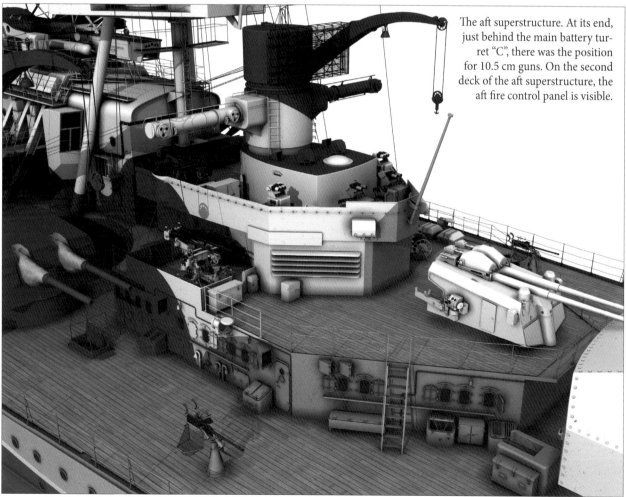

The aft superstructure. At its end, just behind the main battery turret "C", there was the position for 10.5 cm guns. On the second deck of the aft superstructure, the aft fire control panel is visible.

A view of the bow superstructure.

The starboard side of the aft superstructure and details of its equipment together with a double position for of the 37 mm guns.

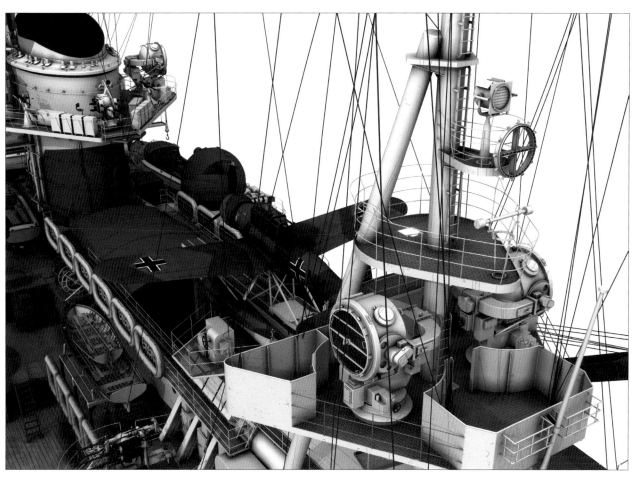

The central part of the aft mast with a visible platform for reflectors with a mirror diameter of 1.6 metres.

A view of the battleship's stern with the turret "C" of the 28 cm main battery visible from the rear.

A shot of the front of main battery turret "C" visible from the starboard side and equipment of the aft part of the main deck.

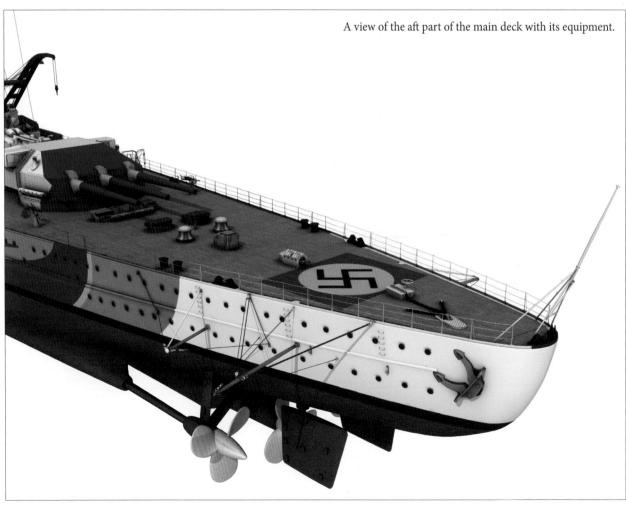

A view of the aft part of the main deck with its equipment.

The top view of the amidships of the battleship with a visible part of the command tower.

The port side view of a fragment of the bow superstructure with a visible SL-6 fire control position and anti-aircraft battery.

The starboard fore view of the
hangar and the three-legged
aft mast. The ship's rigging is
clearly visible.

A view from the starboard of a part of the command tower and the funnel. The painting the ship as of September 1943.

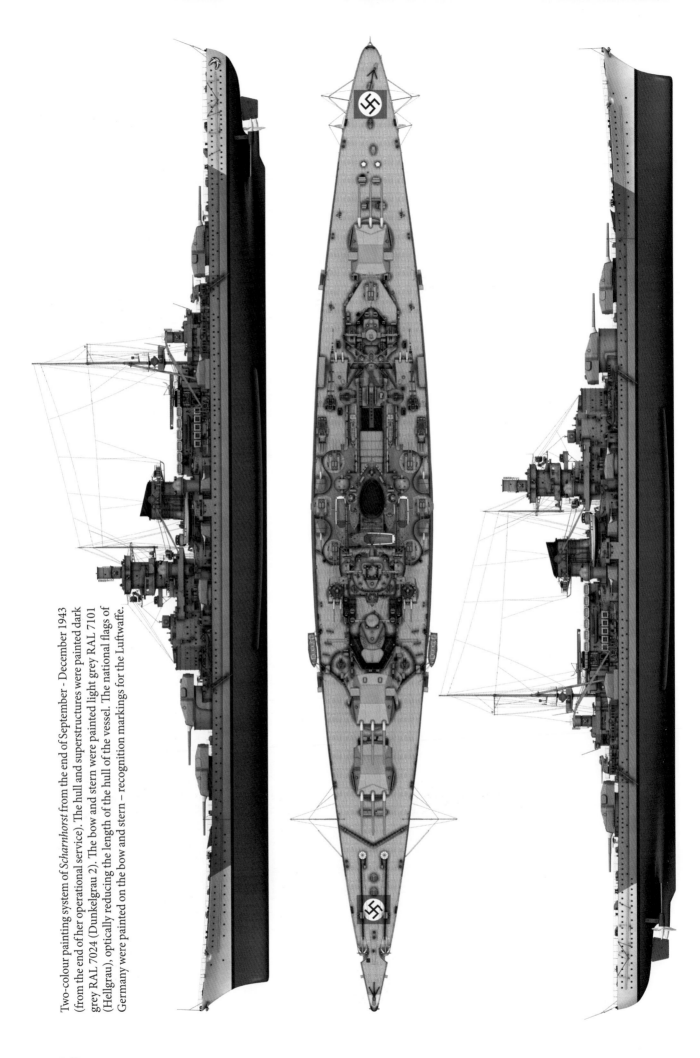

Two-colour painting system of *Scharnhorst* from the end of September - December 1943 (from the end of her operational service). The hull and superstructures were painted dark grey RAL 7024 (Dunkelgrau 2). The bow and stern were painted light grey RAL 7101 (Hellgrau), optically reducing the length of the hull of the vessel. The national flags of Germany were painted on the bow and stern – recognition markings for the Luftwaffe.

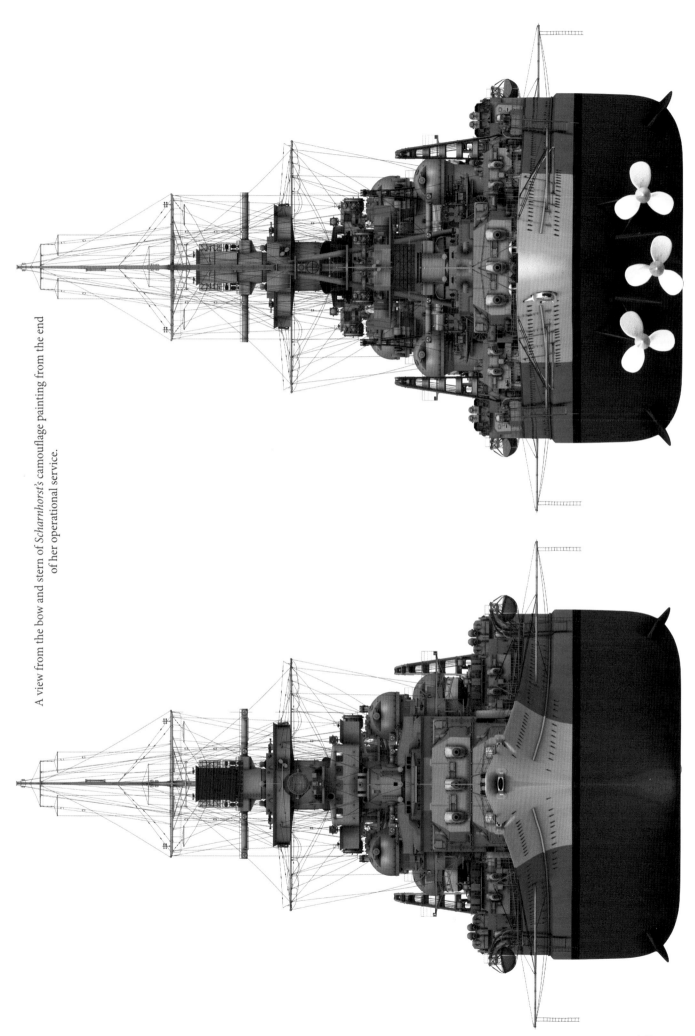

A view from the bow and stern of *Scharnhorst's* camouflage painting from the end of her operational service.

Scharnhorst painted at the end of her operational service.

Scharnhorst painted at the end of her operational service.

Scharnhorst's painting from the end of September - December 1943, the starboard view from the bow.

Scharnhorst's painting from the end of September - December 1943 (the port view from the bow).

The starboard view of the stern part of the battleship.

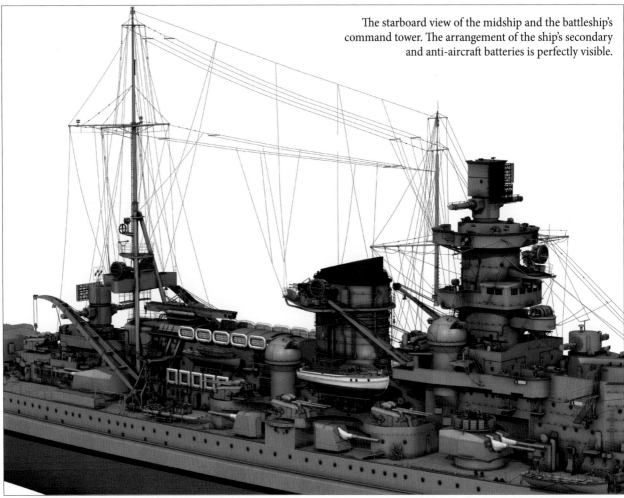

The starboard view of the midship and the battleship's command tower. The arrangement of the ship's secondary and anti-aircraft batteries is perfectly visible.

A view from the port side of the battleship
Scharnhorst in the camouflage painting from 1943.

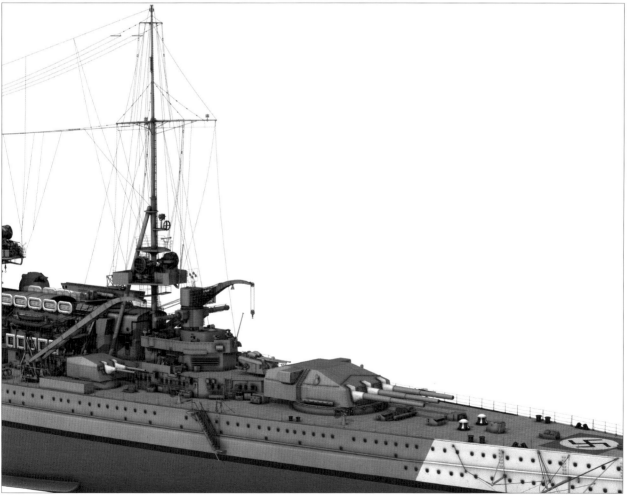

The bow of the battleship in the camouflage painting from 1943.

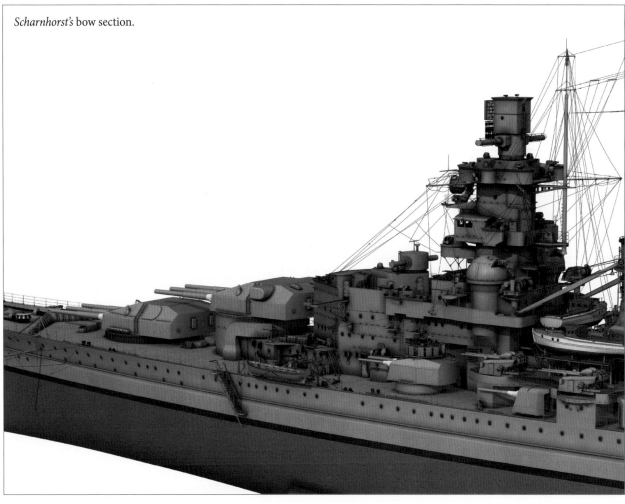

Scharnhorst's bow section.

The battleship's bow. The anchor chains and half-hawseholes are visible.

A view of the bow of the battleship and its equipment.

A view from the bow deck of the main battery turrets and the bow superstructure.

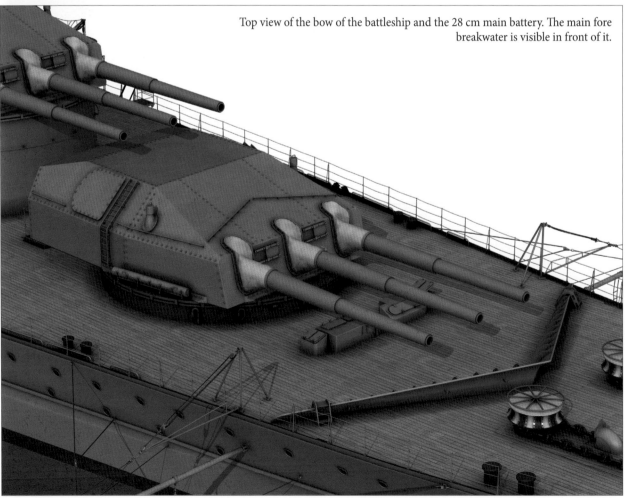

Top view of the bow of the battleship and the 28 cm main battery. The main fore breakwater is visible in front of it.

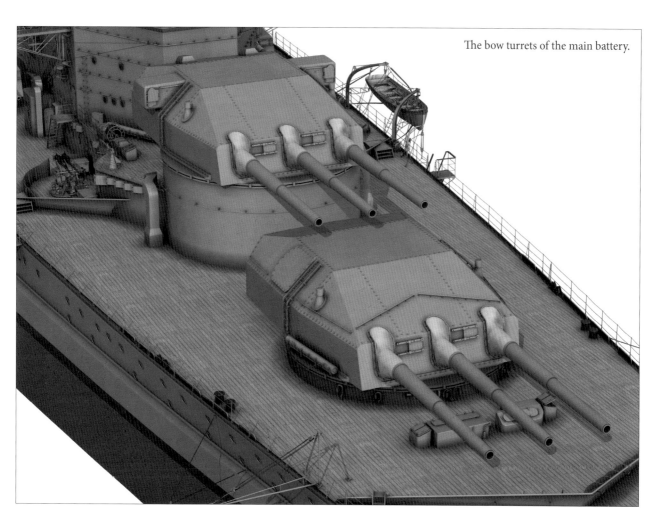

The bow turrets of the main battery.

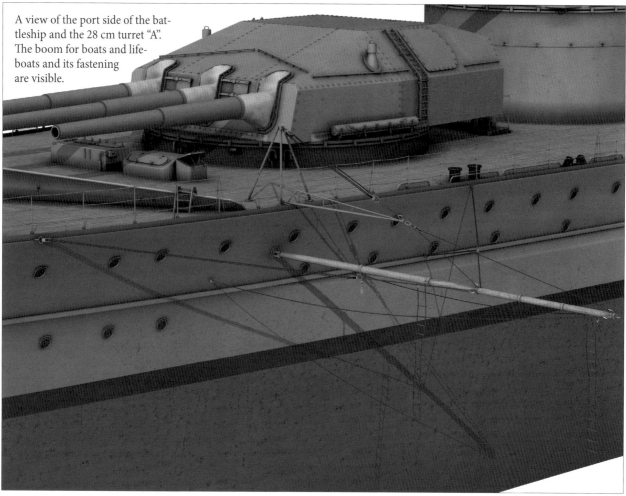

A view of the port side of the battleship and the 28 cm turret "A". The boom for boats and lifeboats and its fastening are visible.

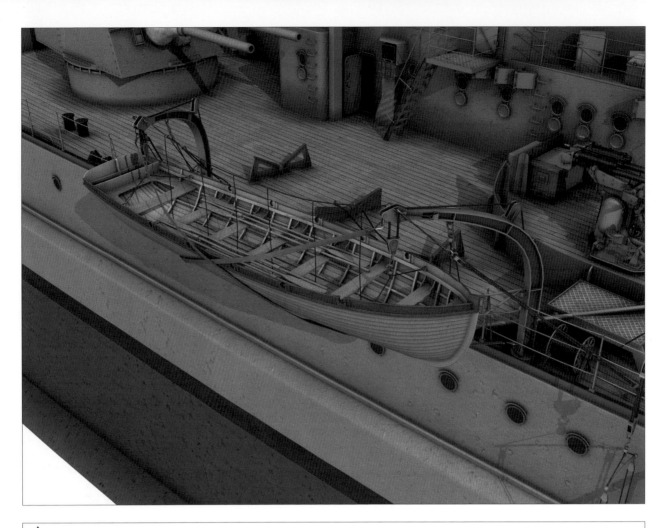

The method of mounting the 8-metre cutter on the side davits. The cranes are located at the level of the side walls of the bow superstructure.

The top view of the davits and the attachment of the 8-metre cutter on the starboard side.

The 8-metre-long cutter mounted on the side davits in fore and aft views.

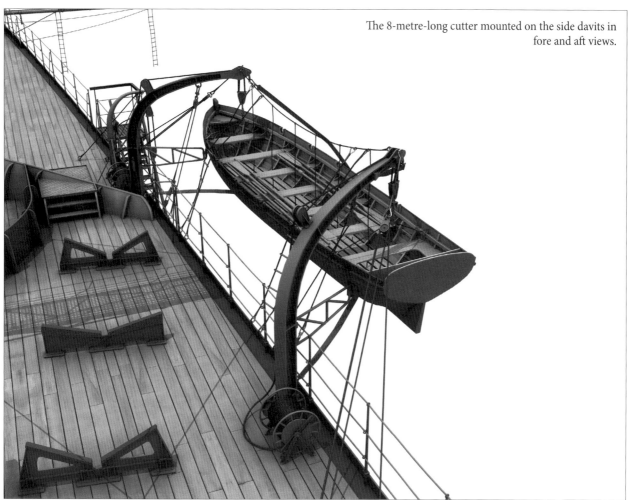

Fixing the cutter on the davit.

The starboard view from the stern of the
upper part of the fore superstructure.

A view of the rear part of the bow superstructure.

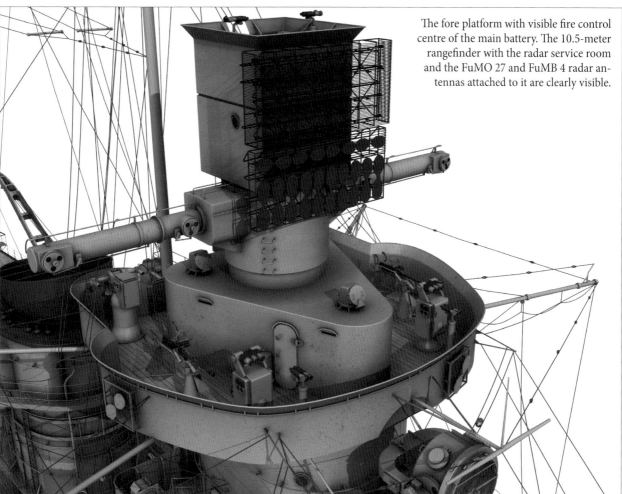

The fore platform with visible fire control centre of the main battery. The 10.5-meter rangefinder with the radar service room and the FuMO 27 and FuMB 4 radar antennas attached to it are clearly visible.

A reflector platform with reflector with a mirror diameter of 1.6 metres placed on it, one of the five the battleship was equipped with.

A view of the bow superstructure and its upper part with platforms. The control position of the main and secondary batteries is clearly visible.

The starboard view of the command tower showing the exact appearance and equipment of the admiral's deck and the searchlight platform.

A detailed view of the built-up admiral's bridge with the equipment next to it. In the first period of her service, *Scharnhorst* had an open bridge.

The amidships of the battleship between the bow superstructure and the funnel. In the foreground, there is a crane to operate communication boats and the type SL-6 fire control station.

A view from the stern of the funnel: the arrangement of the supports for the funnel platform and the artillery and optical equipment mounted on it.

The base of the funnel seen from the bow. On both sides and at the front of the funnel base, communication boats were placed on the joists.

A close-up of one of the three 11-metre communication boats on the ship. The boarded deck cover and wooden structure of the wheelhouse are visible.

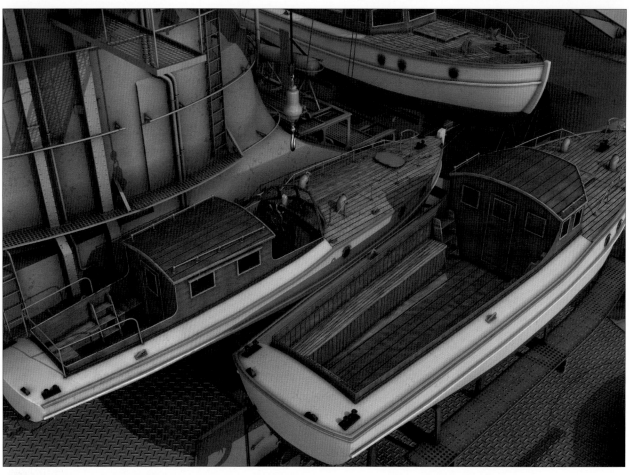

A view of the 11 m long communication boat, behind it you can see the 9 m captain's boat.

The 11-metre communication boat (Verkehrsboot). In the background, you can see a 9.2-metre-long motor cutter.

A 10.5 cm training cannon with a shortened barrel.

A view of the port-side position for the 10.5 cm guns, right behind it, there is an anti-aircraft fire control post model SL-6. In the lower-left corner, you can see a single 15 cm cannon.

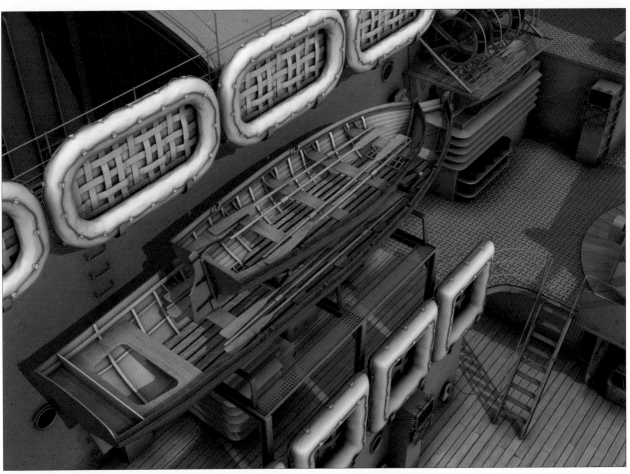

A 8-metre-long lifeboat set on joists on the deck of the aft superstructure at the height of the hangar. There is a 5-metre-long yawl on it.

Details of the liferaft assembly and boat placement near the hangar.

184

A close-up of the upper rear part of the hangar, on which a 14 m long catapult for on-board seaplanes was put.

A view from the stern to the left side of the aft superstructure. The equipment details are clearly visible.

The starboard aft view.

The midship of the battleship.

The aft superstructure with its full equipment.

The aft superstructure.

A platform for the aft mast searchlights. The arrangement of the platform supports is perfectly visible.

The aftdeck with its equipment.

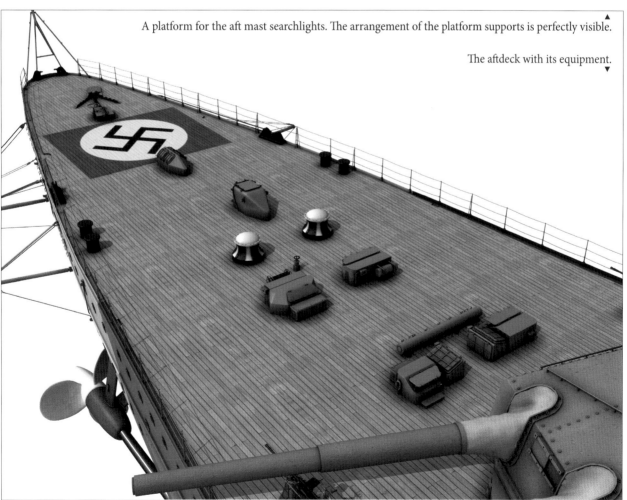

Part of the deck in front of the turret Caesar. Components of the equipment located in this part of the deck are highly visible.

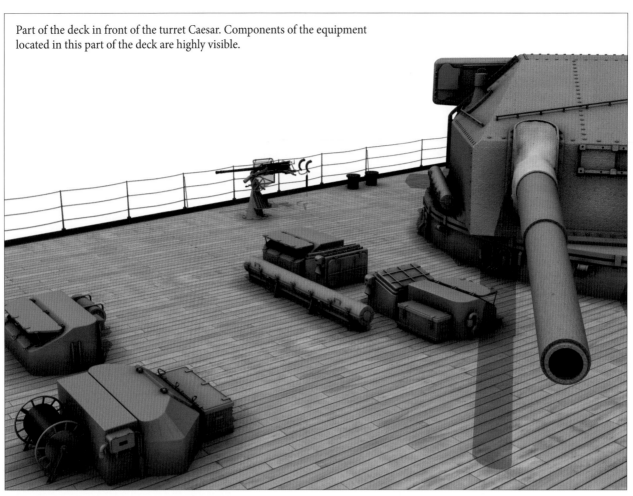

A view of the port side of the ship from the stern.

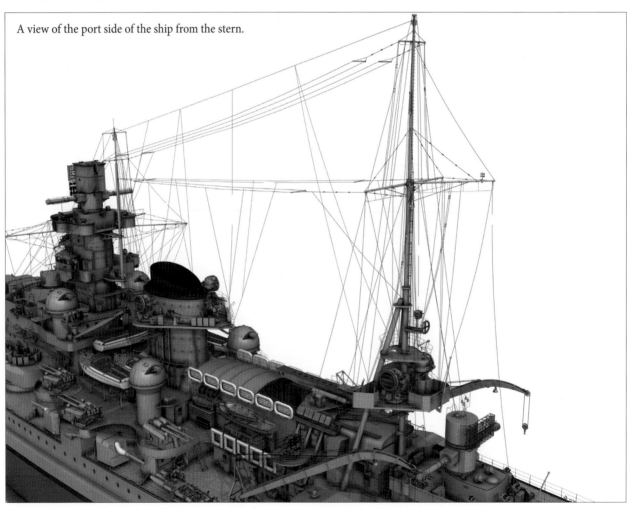

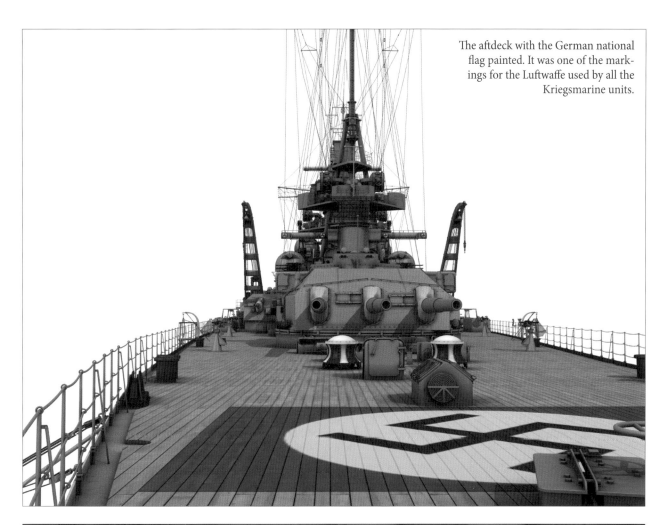

The aftdeck with the German national flag painted. It was one of the markings for the Luftwaffe used by all the Kriegsmarine units.

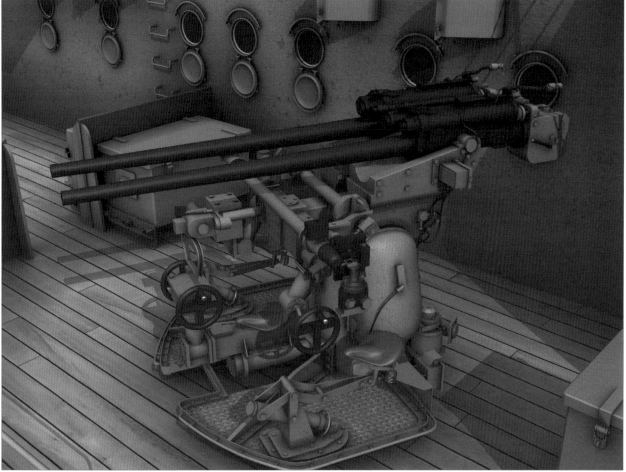

The 3.7 cm anti-aircraft gun model SK C / 30 on the double C / 30 gun.

The 20 mm Flak Vierling C 38 AA gun.

The fast-firing 10.5 cm SK C / 33 heavy anti-aircraft battery cannon mounted on the LC 31 gE double gun carriage.

Access stairs mounted on the aft superstructure near the main battery turret "C".

The descent gangway.

The triple 533mm torpedo launcher. It was dismantled from the cruiser NÜRNBERG and mounted on the battleship during her stay in Brest in 1941.

The rigging between the masts.

Details of ship cranes for handling the Ar-196 seaplanes and ship's boats. The cranes were also used to load supplies.

The command tower with the base of the main mast visible in the foreground and the back of the admiral's platform.

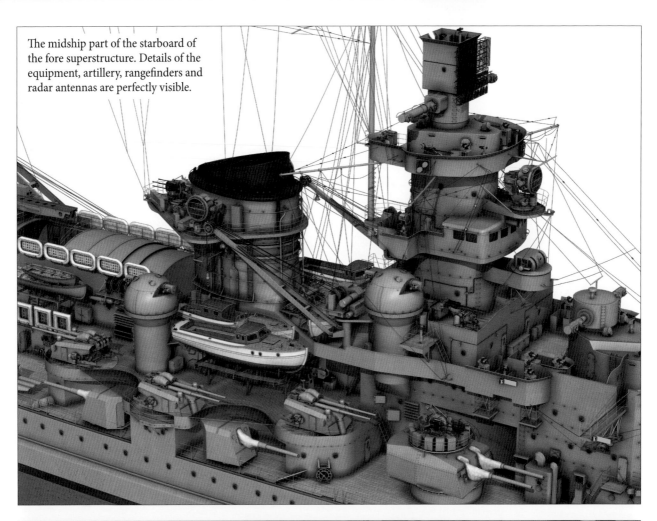

The midship part of the starboard of the fore superstructure. Details of the equipment, artillery, rangefinders and radar antennas are perfectly visible.

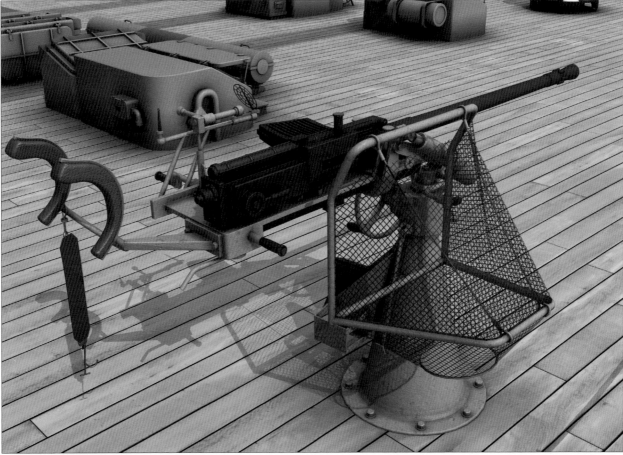

The rear view of the single 20 mm Flak C / 38 AA gun. It is worth paying attention to the visible net used to collect shells from projectiles fired.

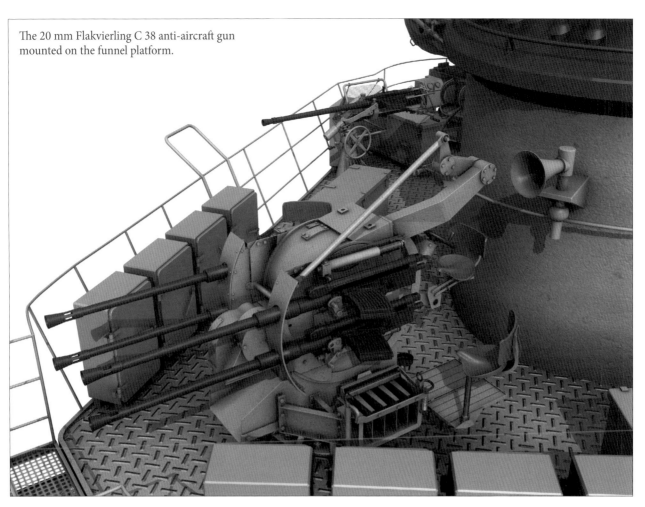

The 20 mm Flakvierling C 38 anti-aircraft gun mounted on the funnel platform.

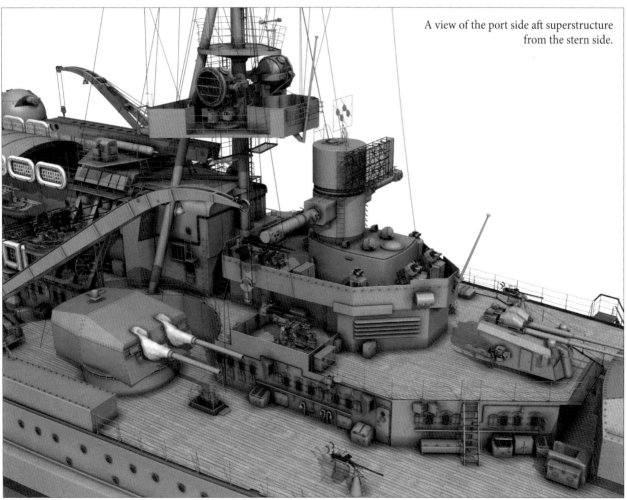

A view of the port side aft superstructure from the stern side.

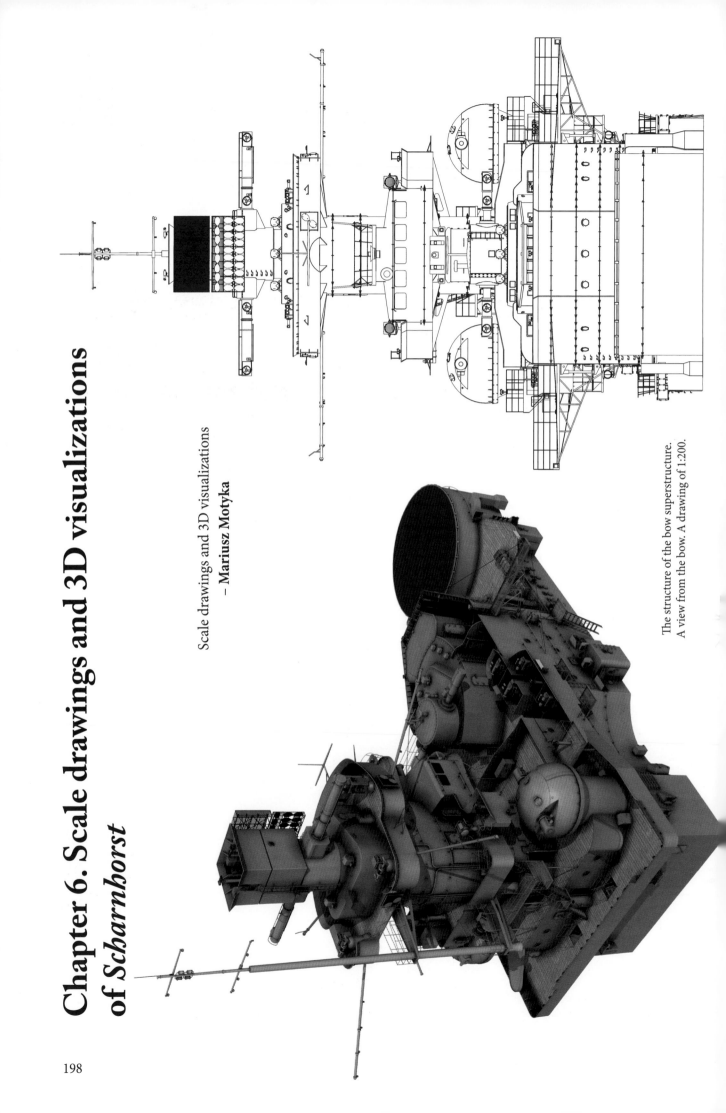

Chapter 6. Scale drawings and 3D visualizations of *Scharnhorst*

Scale drawings and 3D visualizations
– **Mariusz Motyka**

The structure of the bow superstructure.
A view from the bow. A drawing of 1:200.

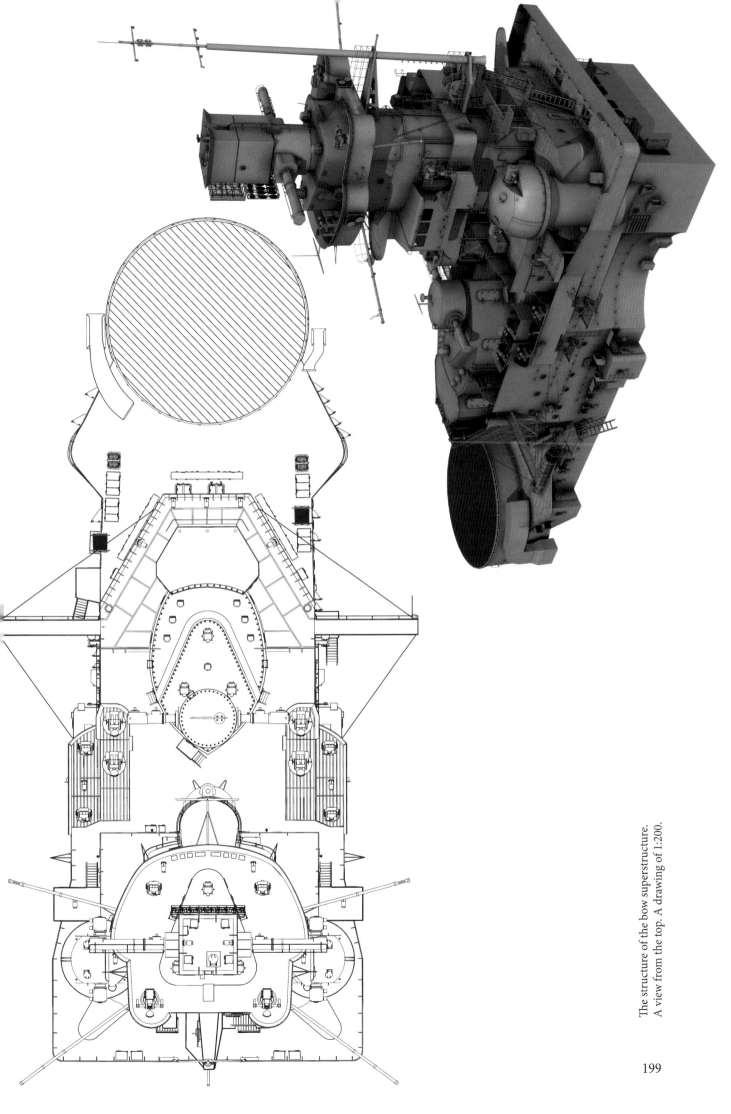

The structure of the bow superstructure.
A view from the top. A drawing of 1:200.

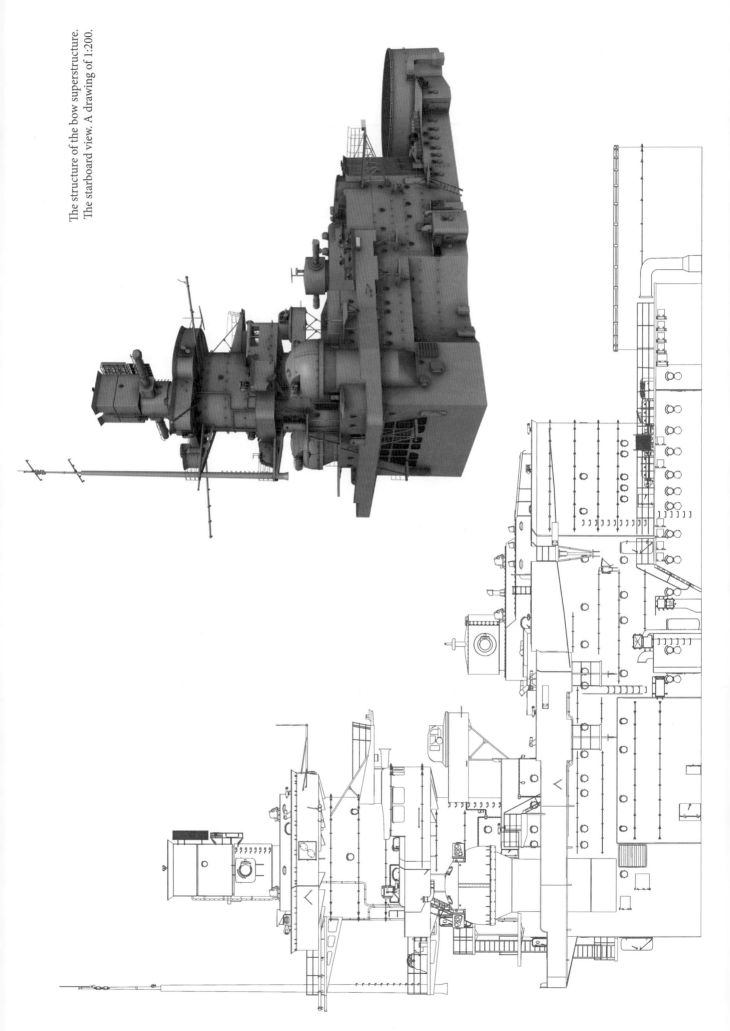

The structure of the bow superstructure.
The starboard view. A drawing of 1:200.

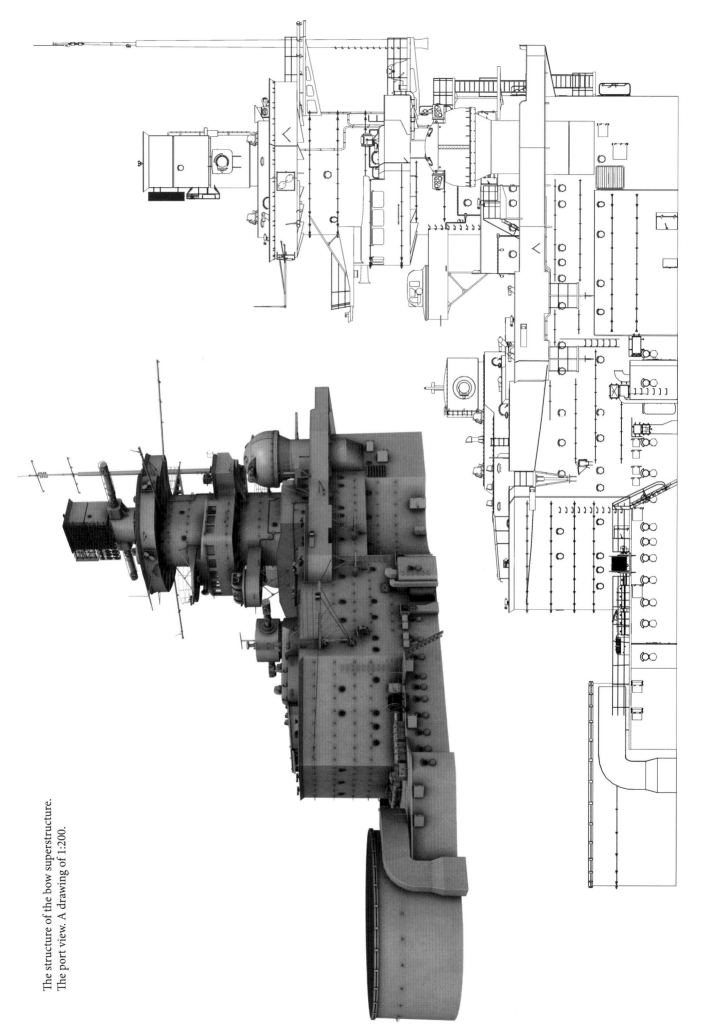

The structure of the bow superstructure.
The port view. A drawing of 1:200.

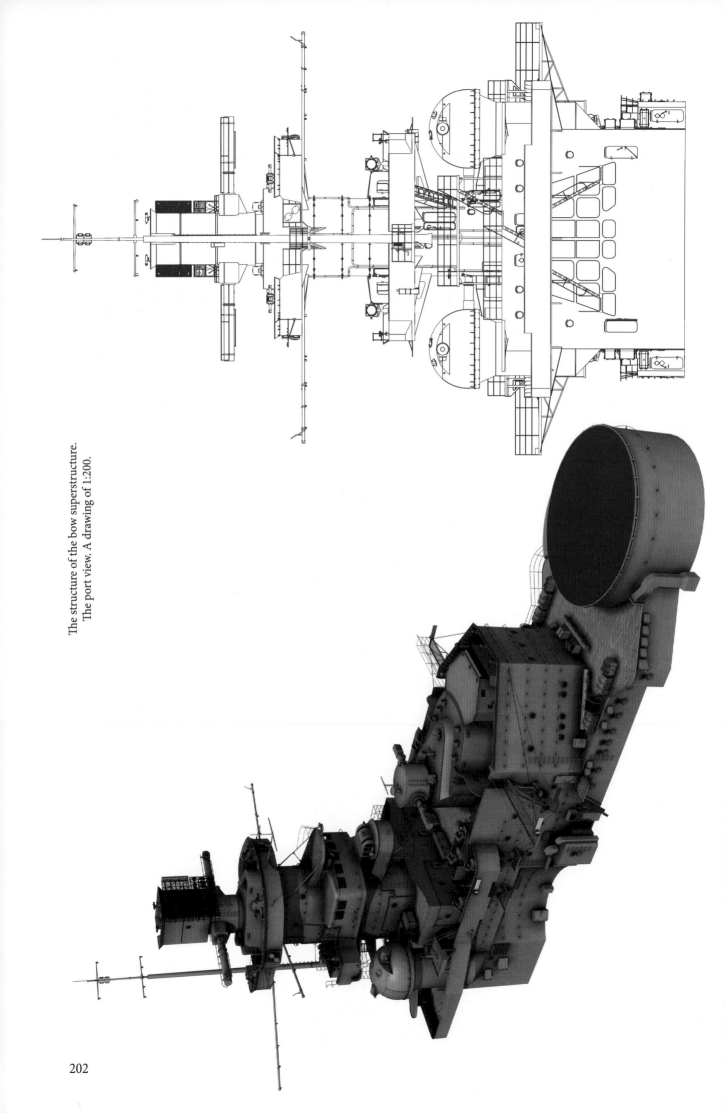

The structure of the bow superstructure.
The port view. A drawing of 1:200.

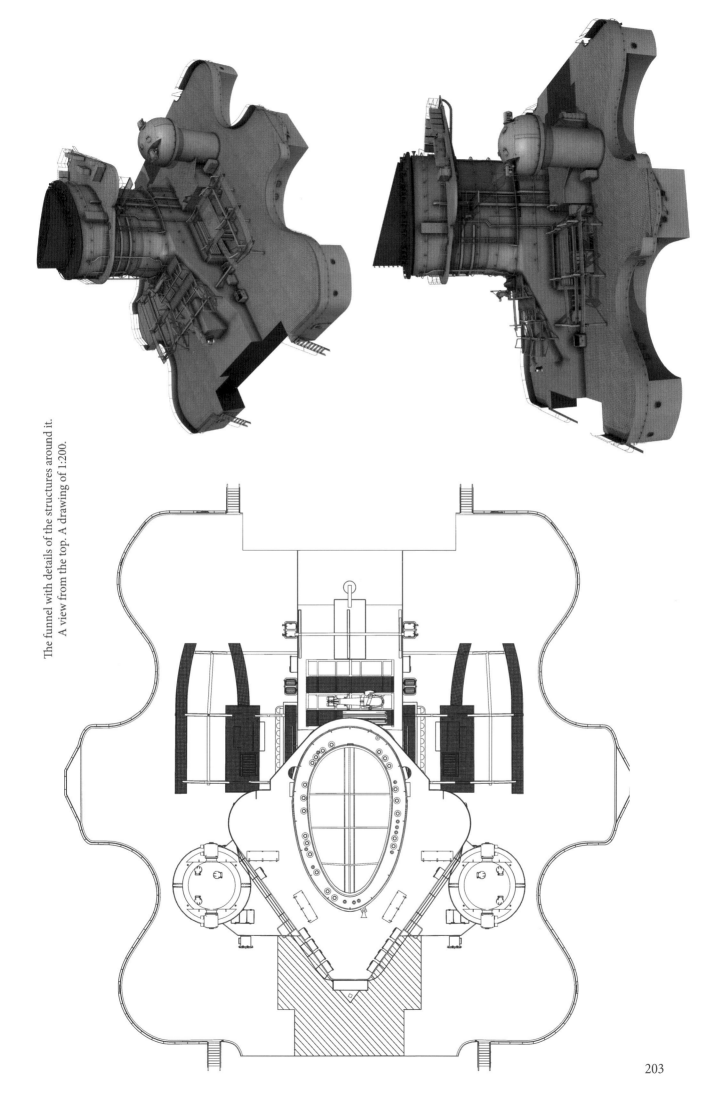

The funnel with details of the structures around it.
A view from the top. A drawing of 1:200.

203

The funnel with details of the structures.
The aft view. A drawing of 1:200.

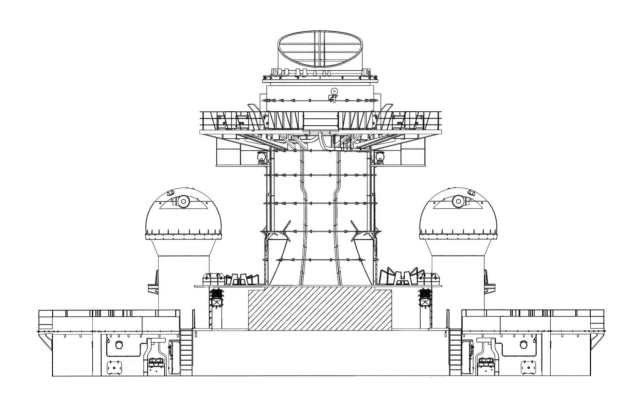

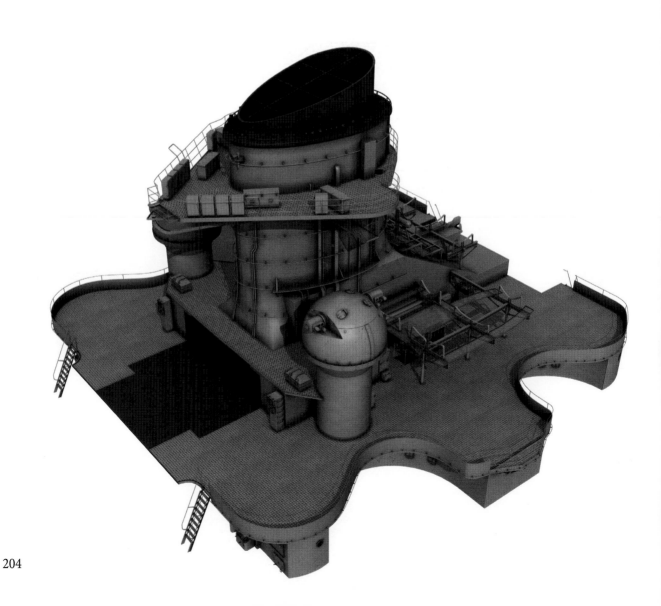

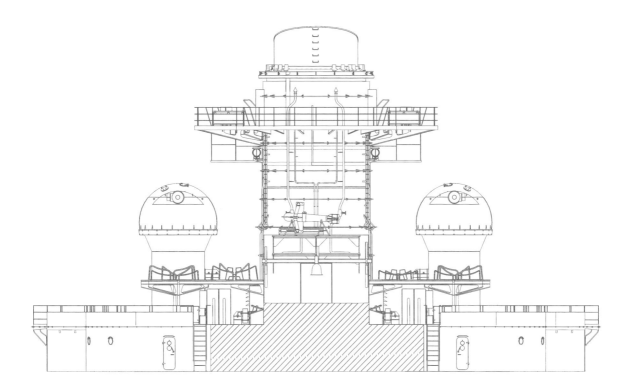

The funnel with details of the structures.
The bow view. A drawing of 1:200.

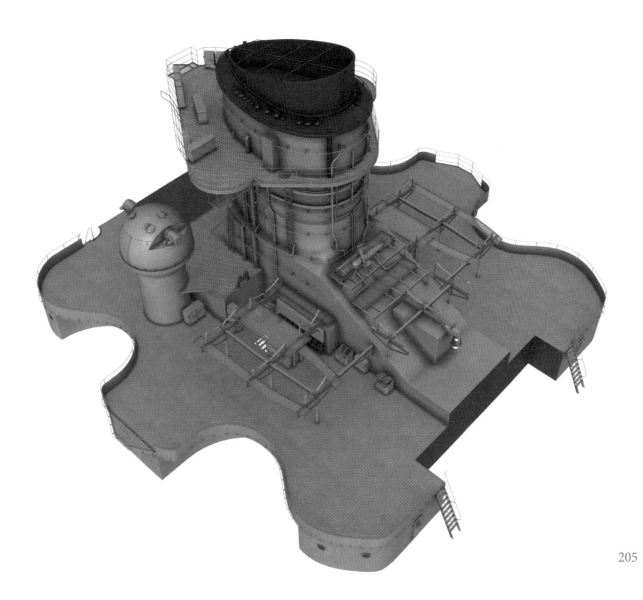

The funnel with details of the structures around it.
The starboard view. A drawing of 1:200.

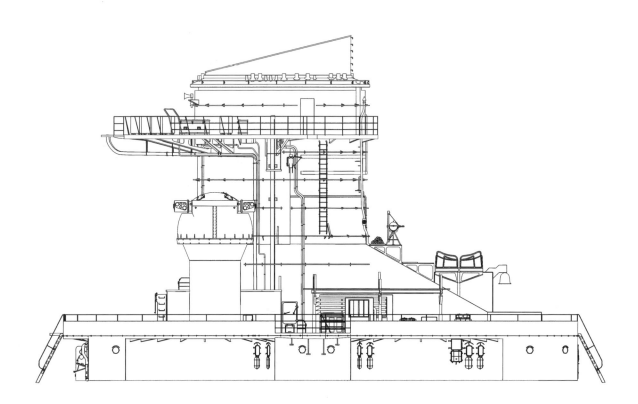

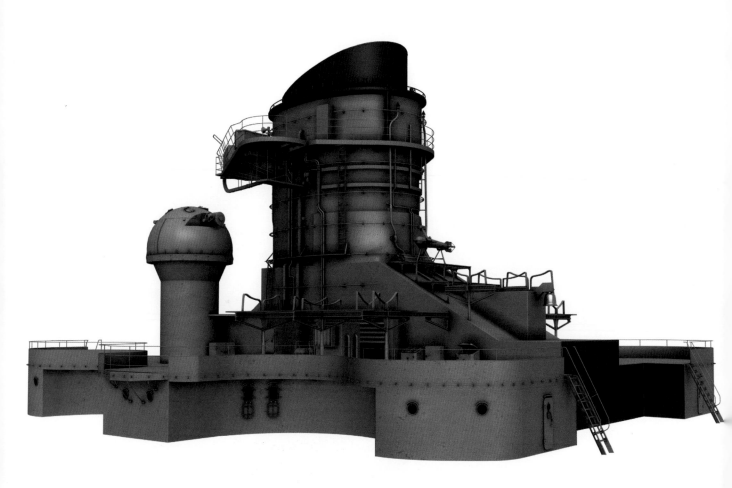

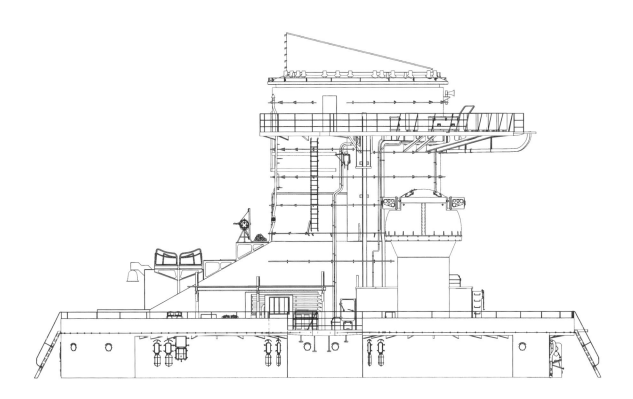

The funnel with details of the buildings around it.
The port view. A drawing of 1:200.

The hangar for on-board seaplanes. Details of the hangar.
A view from above. A drawing of 1:200.

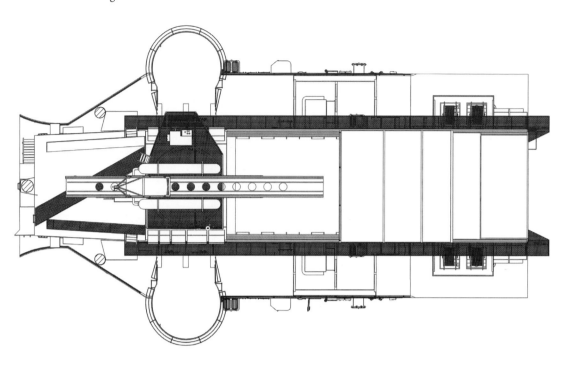

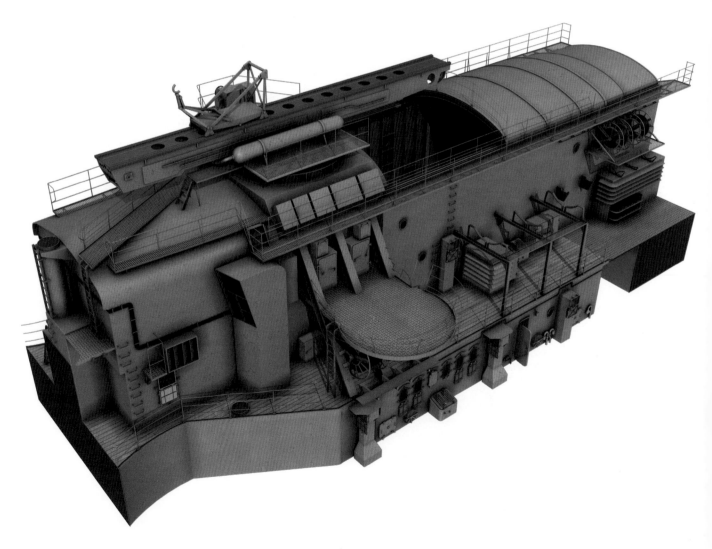

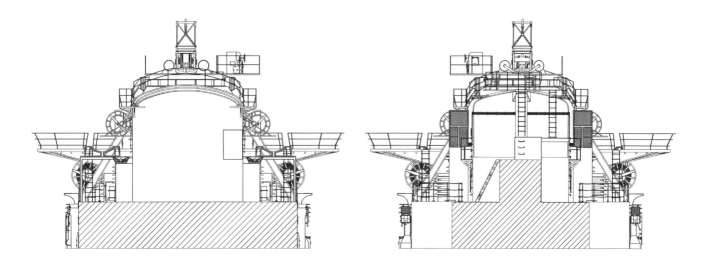

The hangar for on-board seaplanes. Details of the hangar.
The bow and aft views. Drawings of 1:200.

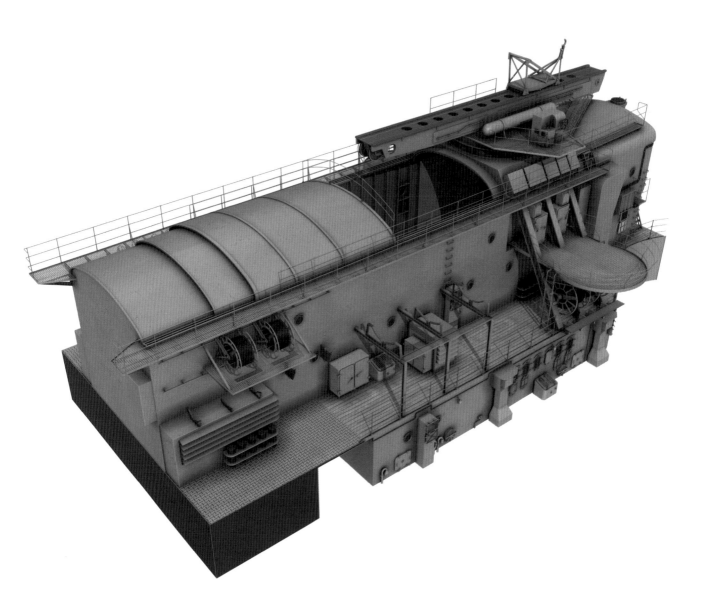

209

The hangar for on-board seaplanes. Details of the hangar.
The starboard view. A drawing of 1:200.

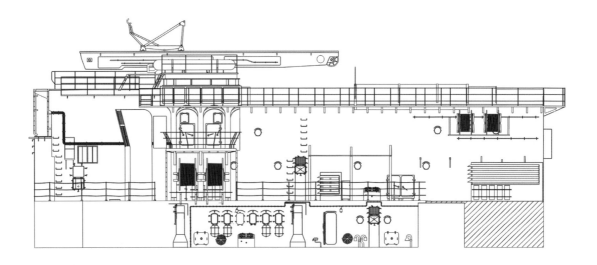

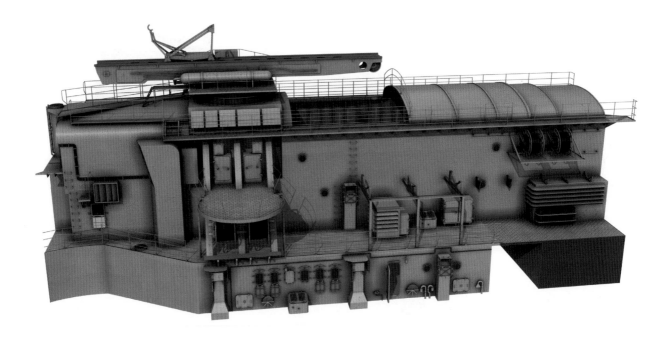

The hangar for on-board seaplanes. Details of the hangar development.
The port side view. A drawing of 1:200.

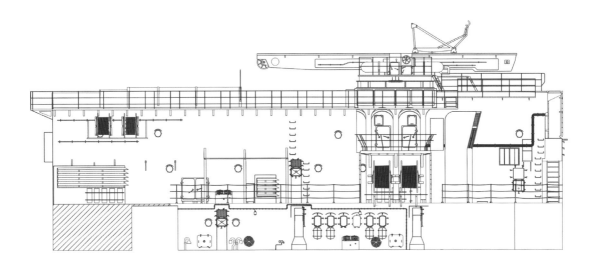

211

The structure of the aft superstructure.
The top view of the superstructure. A drawing of 1:200.

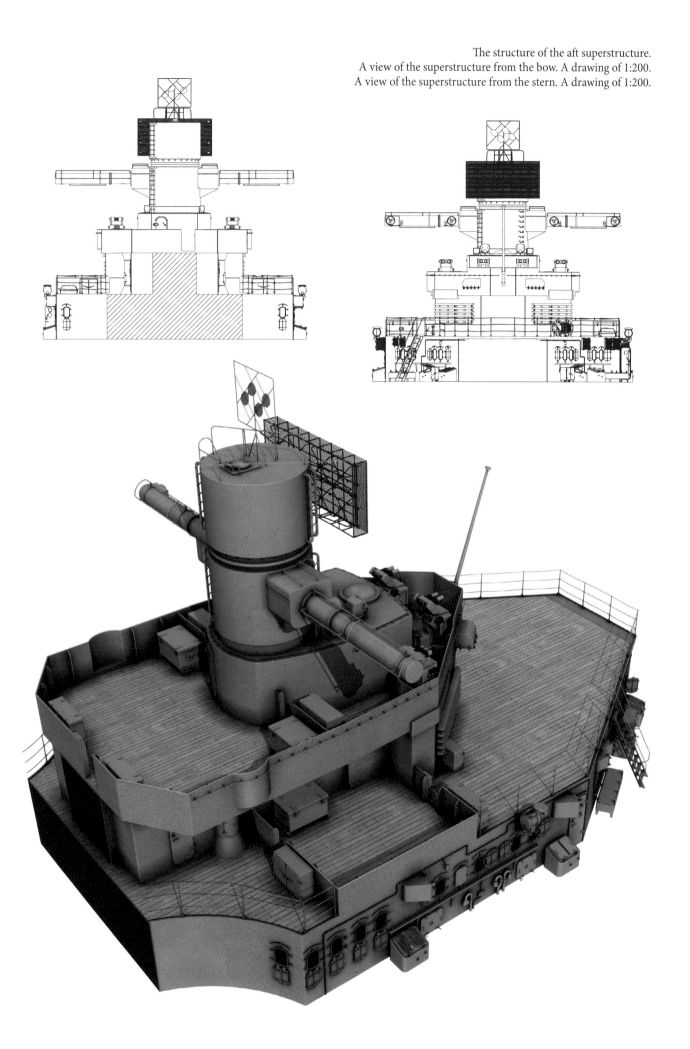

The structure of the aft superstructure.
A view of the superstructure from the bow. A drawing of 1:200.
A view of the superstructure from the stern. A drawing of 1:200.

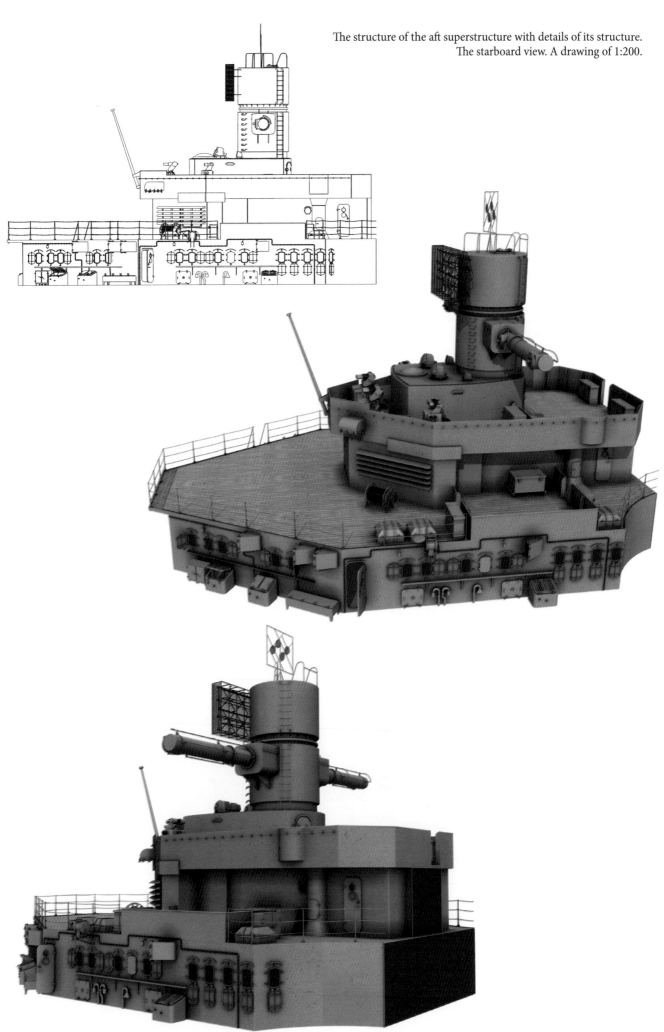

The structure of the aft superstructure with details of its structure.
The starboard view. A drawing of 1:200.

The structure of the aft superstructure with details of the development.
The port view. A drawing of 1:200.

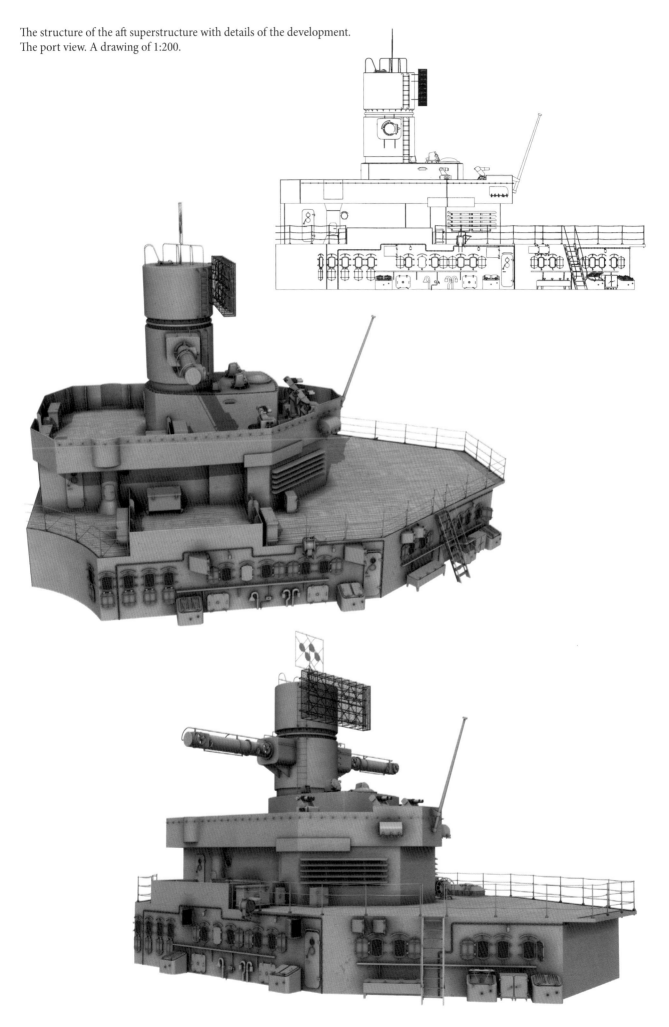

The bow view of the three-legged aft mast (1:200)

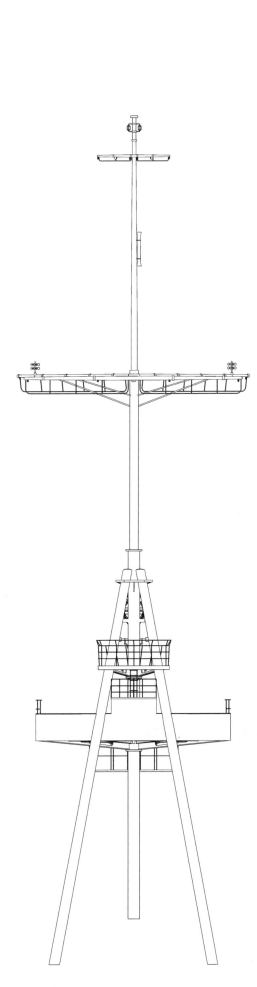

The starboard view of the three-legged aft mast (1:200)

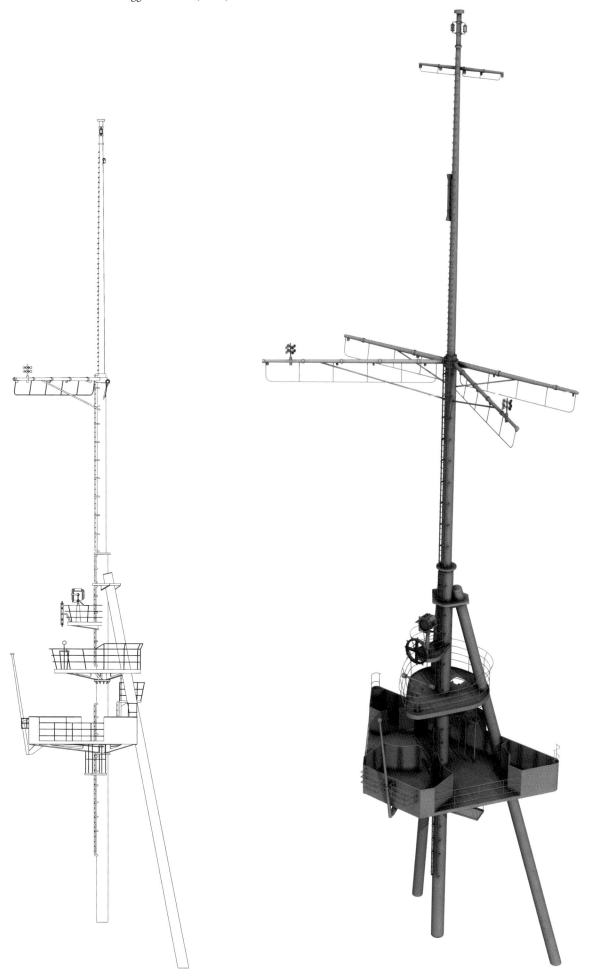

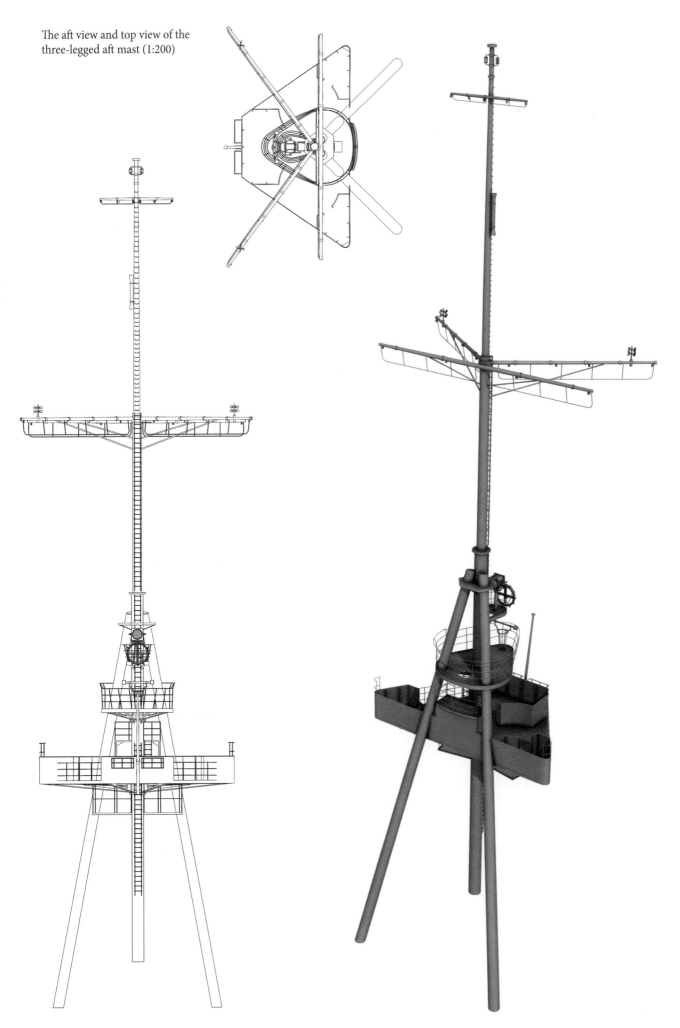

The aft view and top view of the
three-legged aft mast (1:200)

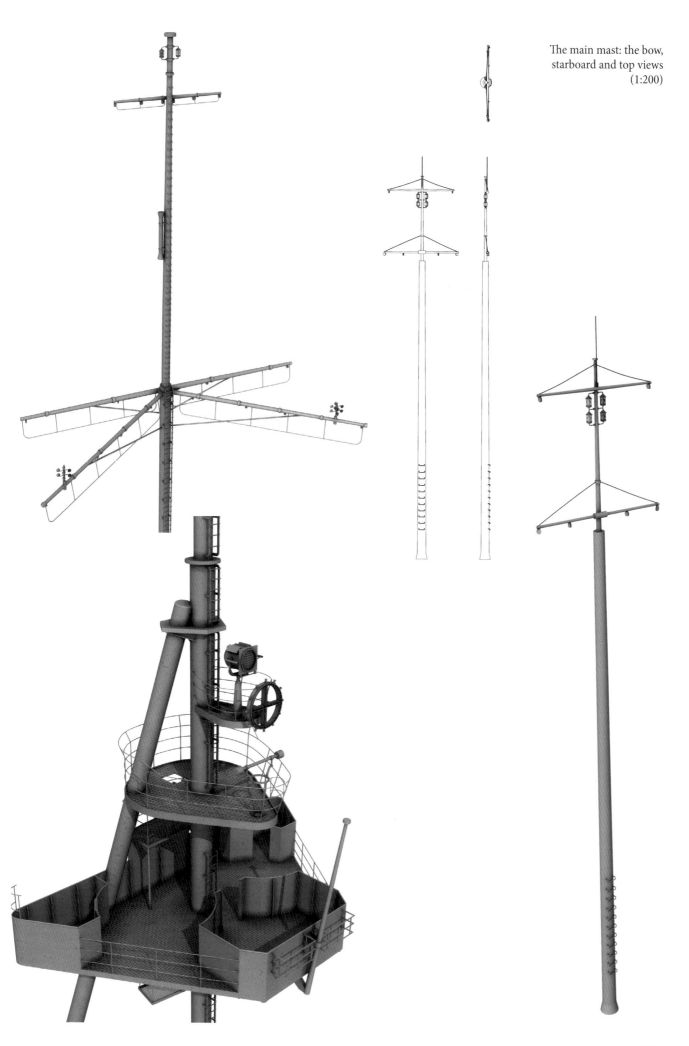

The main mast: the bow,
starboard and top views
(1:200)

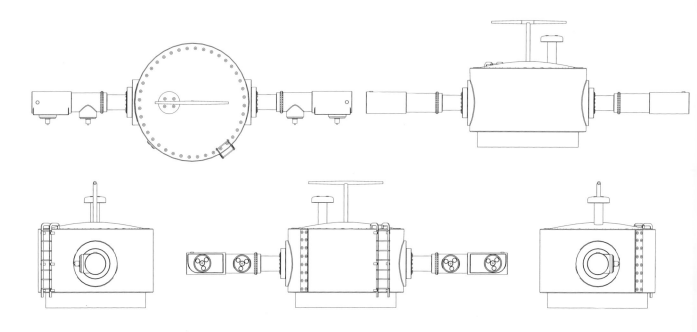

The rangefinder with the base of 6 metres
(1:100).

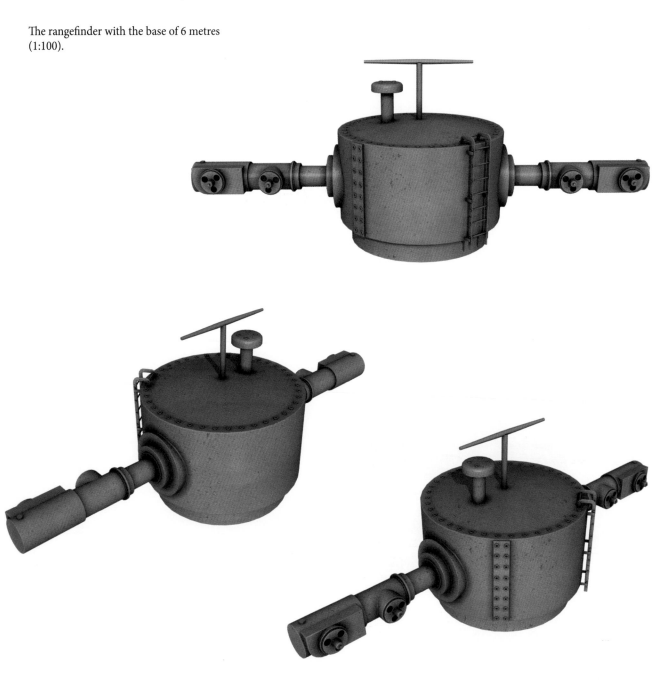

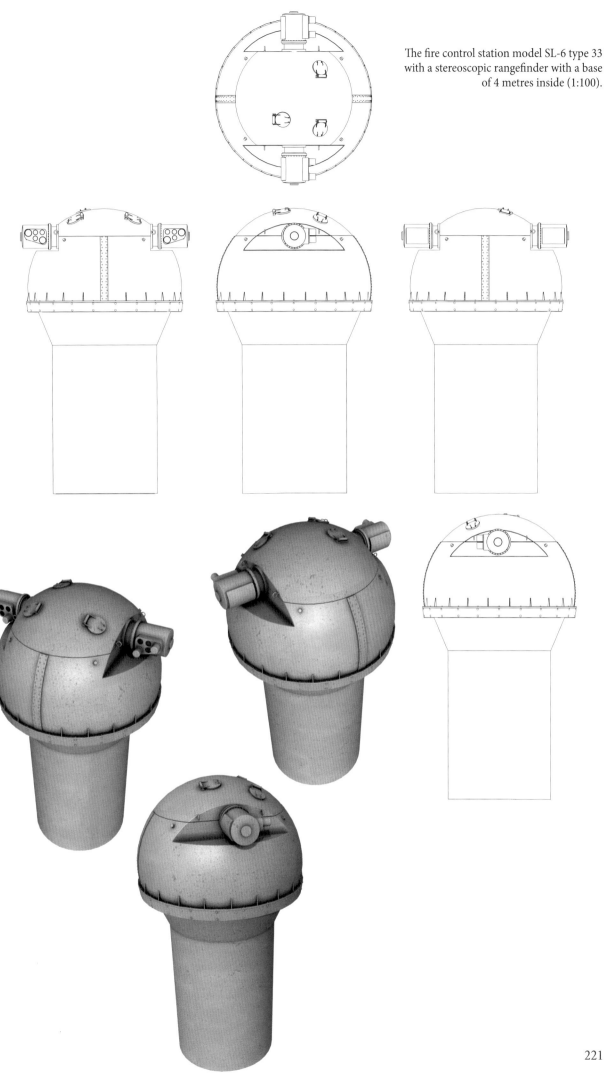

The fire control station model SL-6 type 33 with a stereoscopic rangefinder with a base of 4 metres inside (1:100).

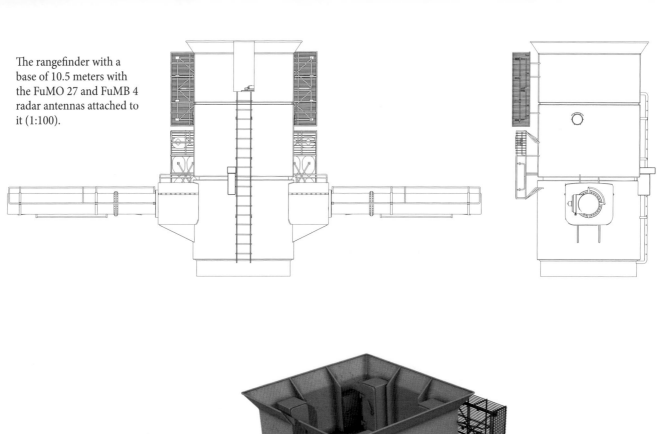

The rangefinder with a base of 10.5 meters with the FuMO 27 and FuMB 4 radar antennas attached to it (1:100).

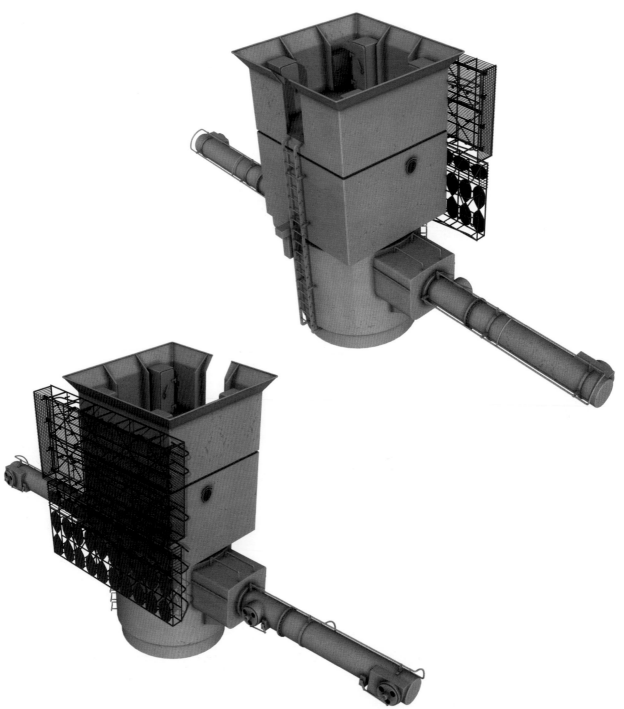

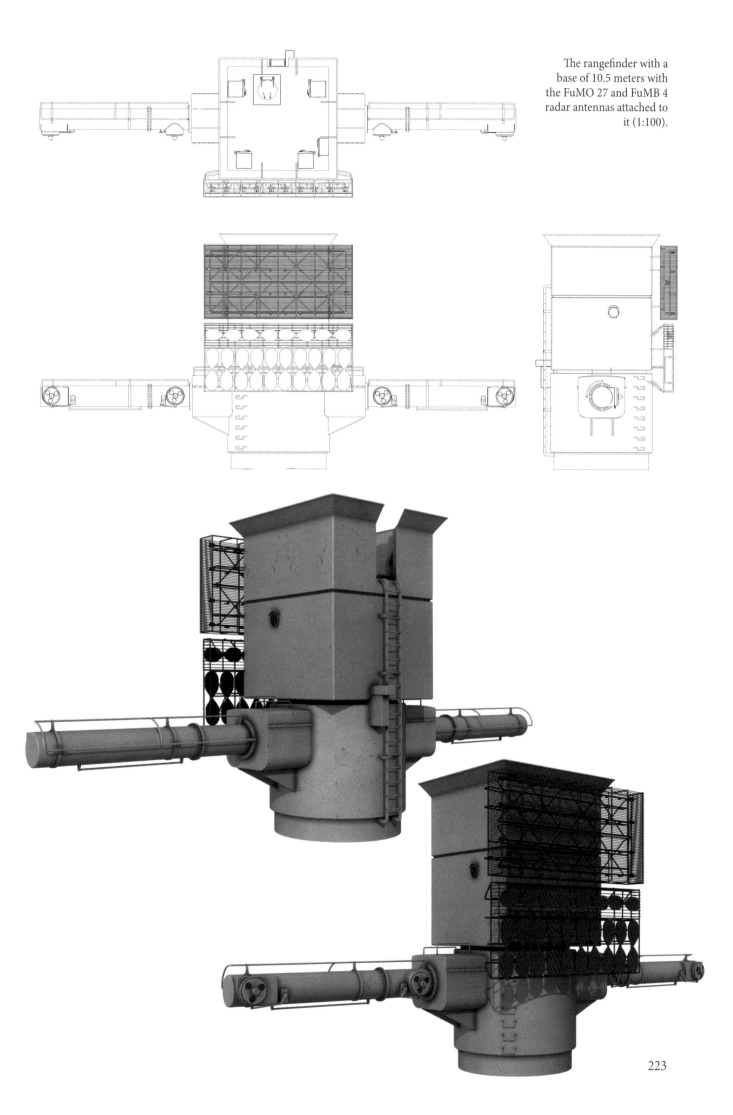

The rangefinder with a base of 10.5 meters with the FuMO 27 and FuMB 4 radar antennas attached to it (1:100).

The rangefinder with a base of 10.5 meters with the FuMO 27 and FuMB 31 ("Palau") radar antennas attached to it (1:100).

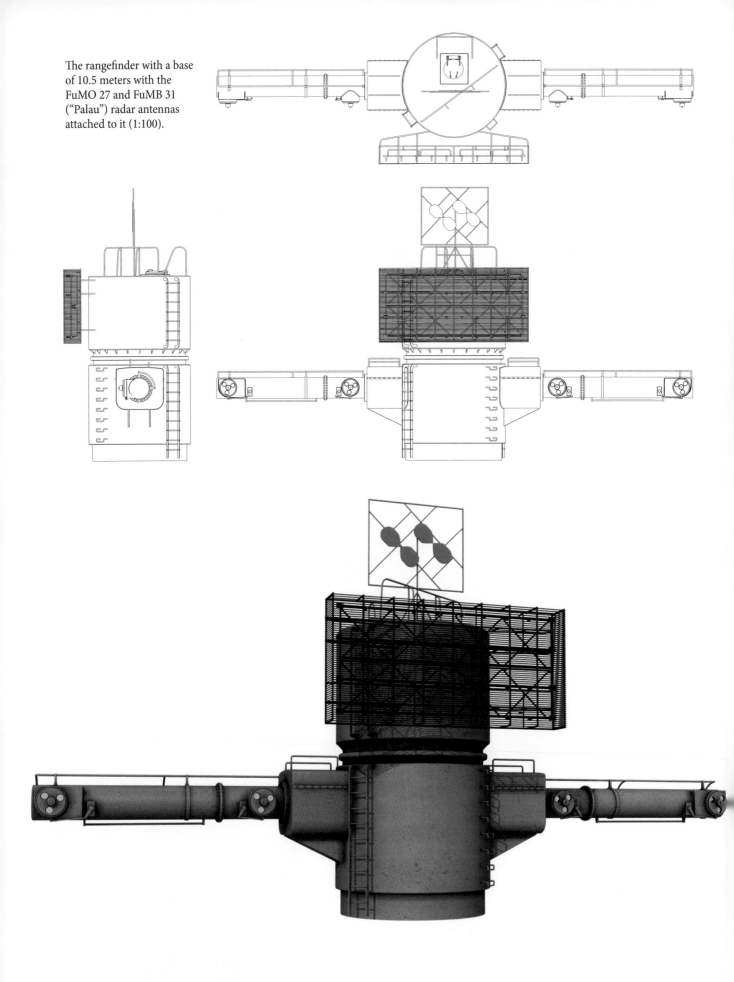

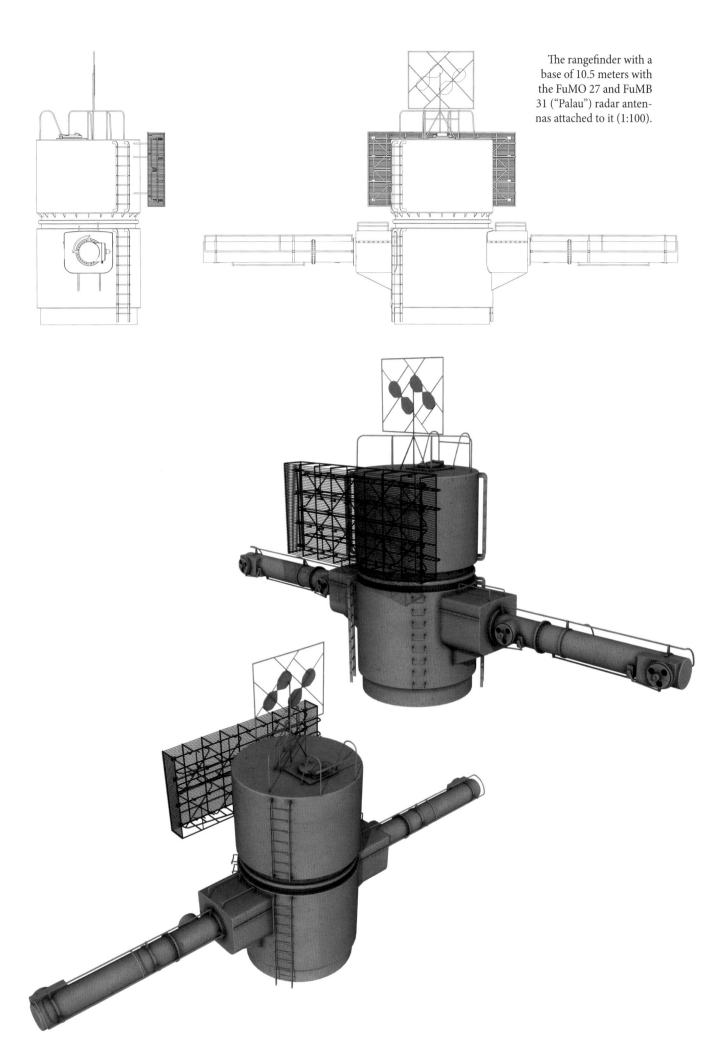

The rangefinder with a base of 10.5 meters with the FuMO 27 and FuMB 31 ("Palau") radar antennas attached to it (1:100).

The rangefinder with a base of 3 meters mounted in a rotating cover (1:50).

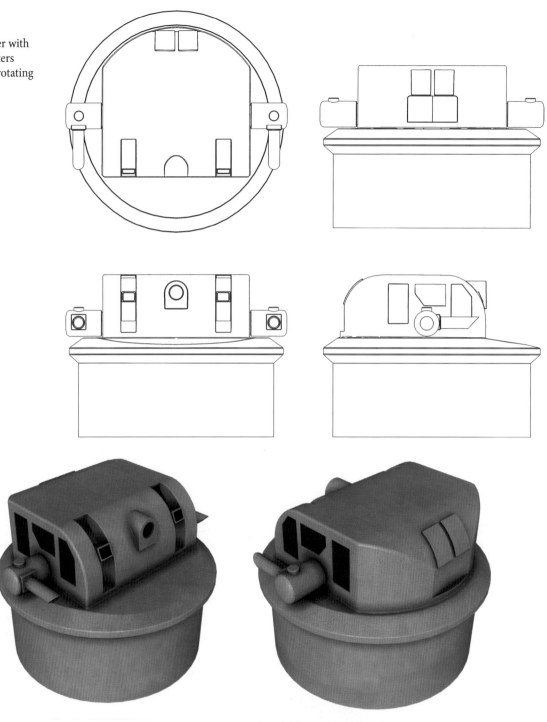

The radar antenna type FuMB 4 ("Sumatra") (1:25).

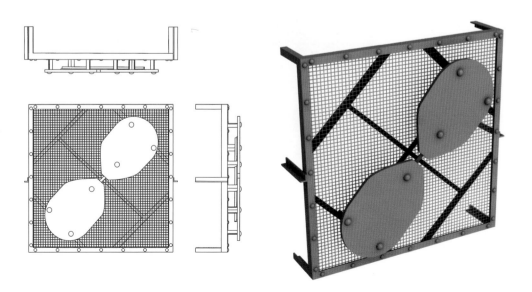

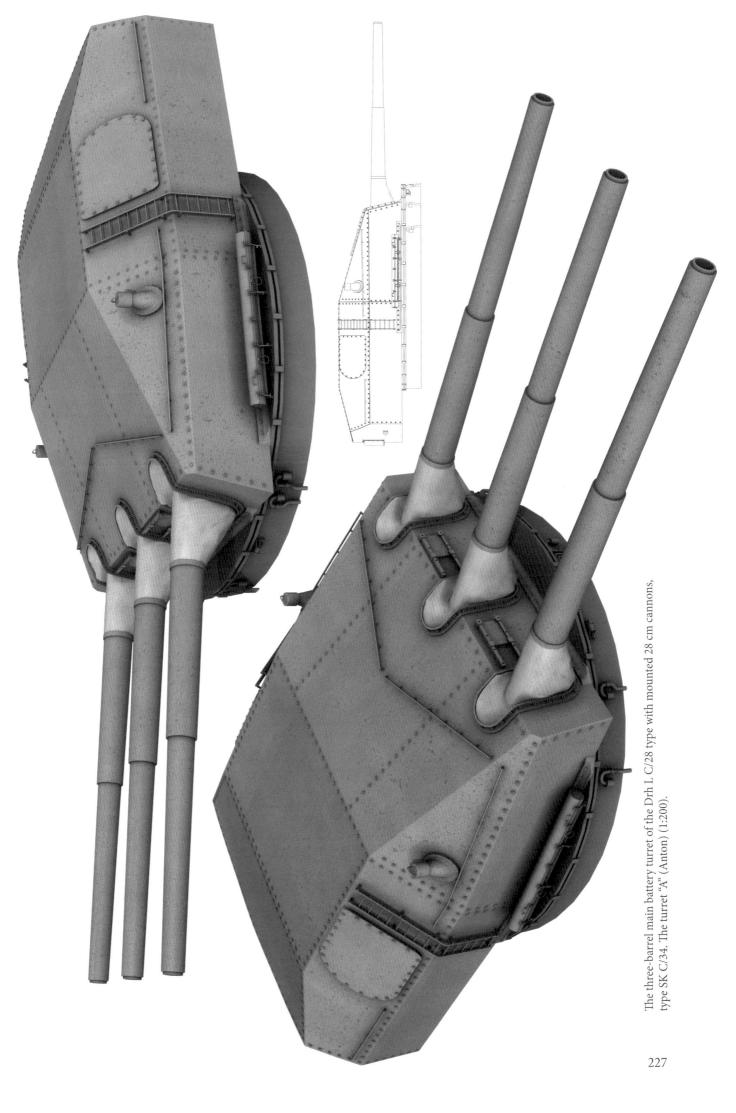

The three-barrel main battery turret of the Drh L C/28 type with mounted 28 cm cannons, type SK C/34. The turret "A" (Anton) (1:200).

227

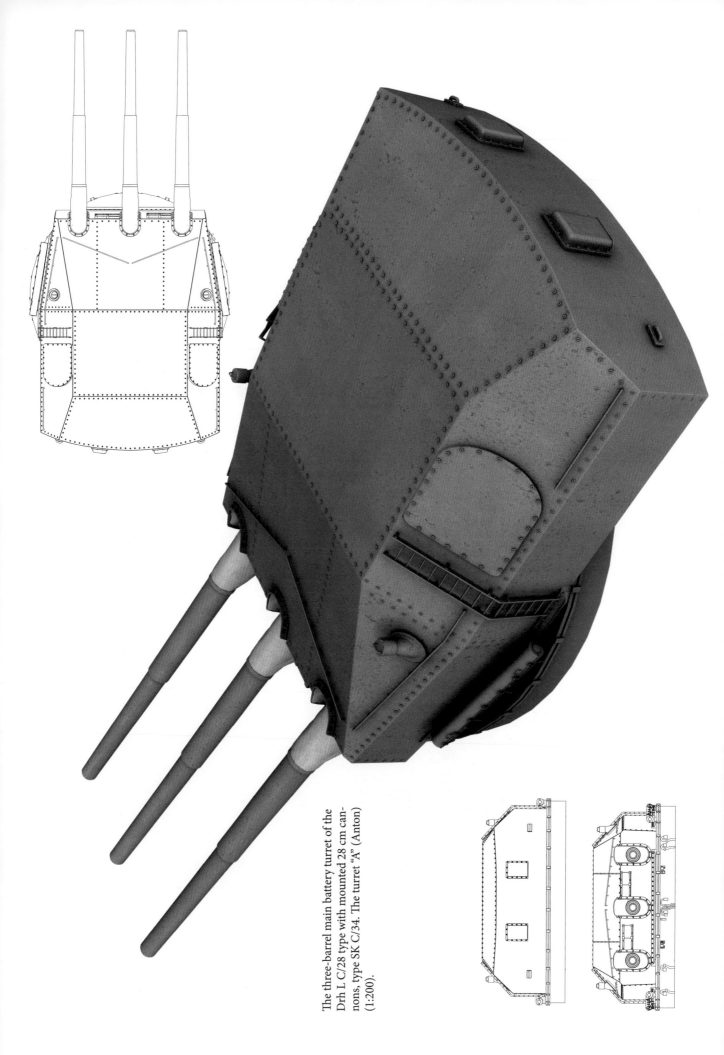

The three-barrel main battery turret of the Drh L C/28 type with mounted 28 cm cannons, type SK C/34. The turret "A" (Anton) (1:200).

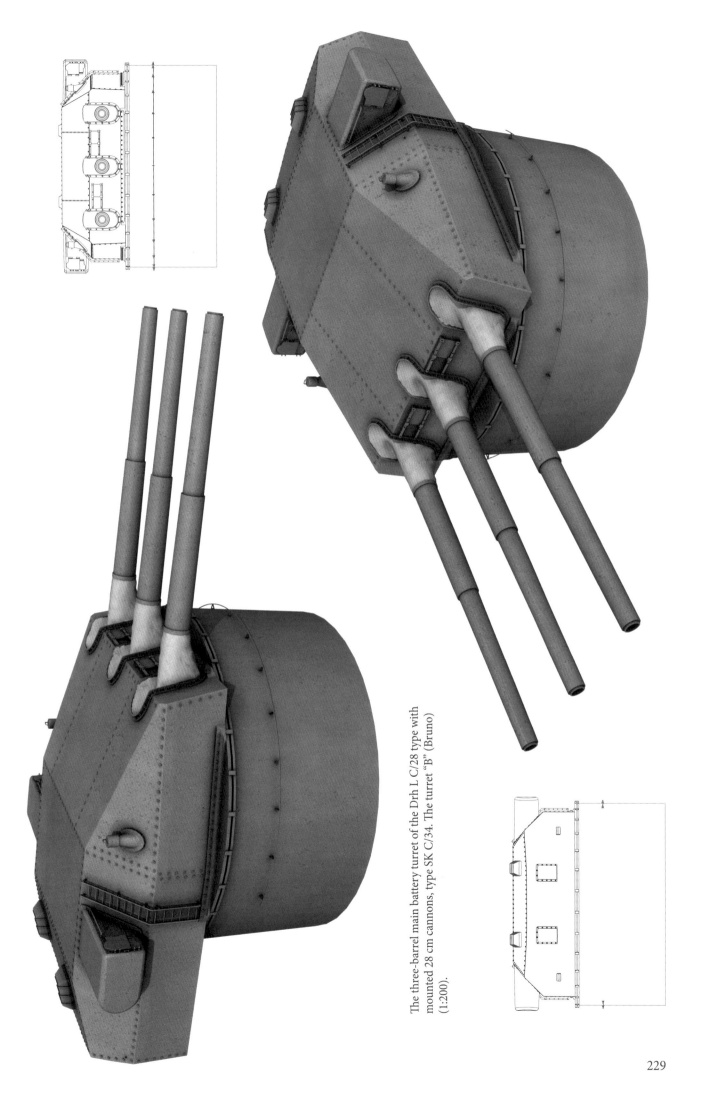

The three-barrel main battery turret of the Drh L C/28 type with mounted 28 cm cannons, type SK C/34. The turret "B" (Bruno) (1:200).

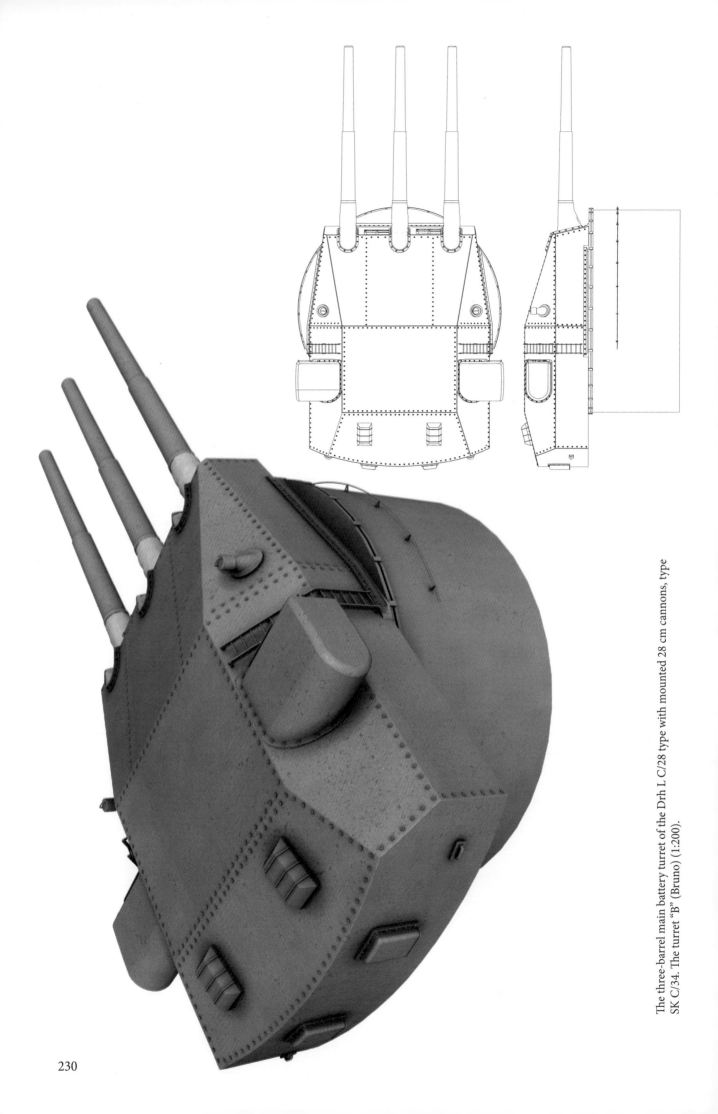

The three-barrel main battery turret of the Drh L C/28 type with mounted 28 cm cannons, type SK C/34. The turret "B" (Bruno) (1:200).

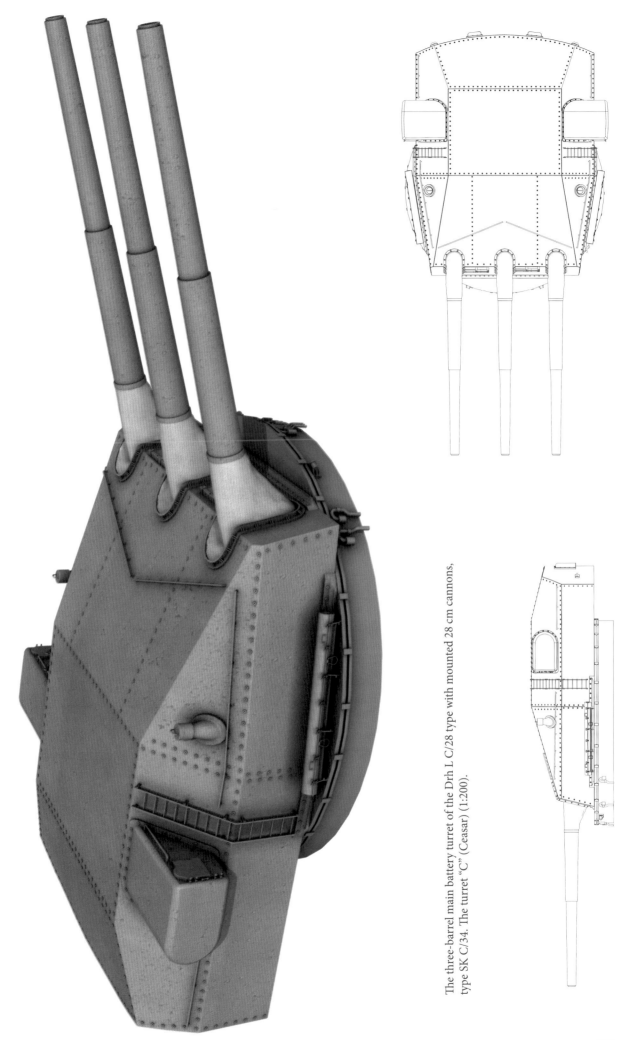

The three-barrel main battery turret of the Drh L C/28 type with mounted 28 cm cannons, type SK C/34. The turret "C" (Ceasar) (1:200).

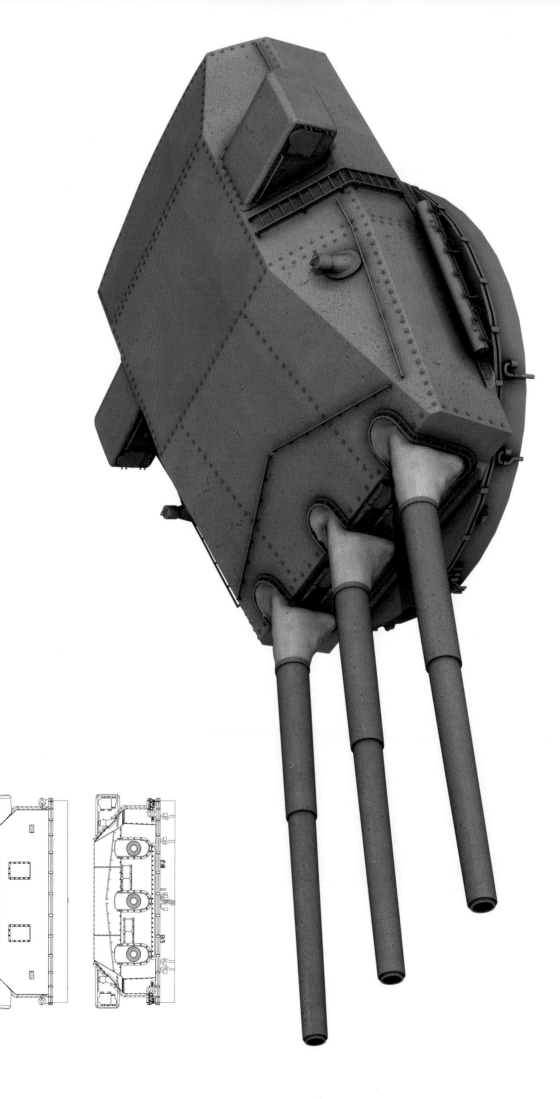

The three-barrel main battery turret of the Drh L C/28 type with mounted 28 cm cannons, type SK C/34. The turret "C" (Ceasar) (1:200).

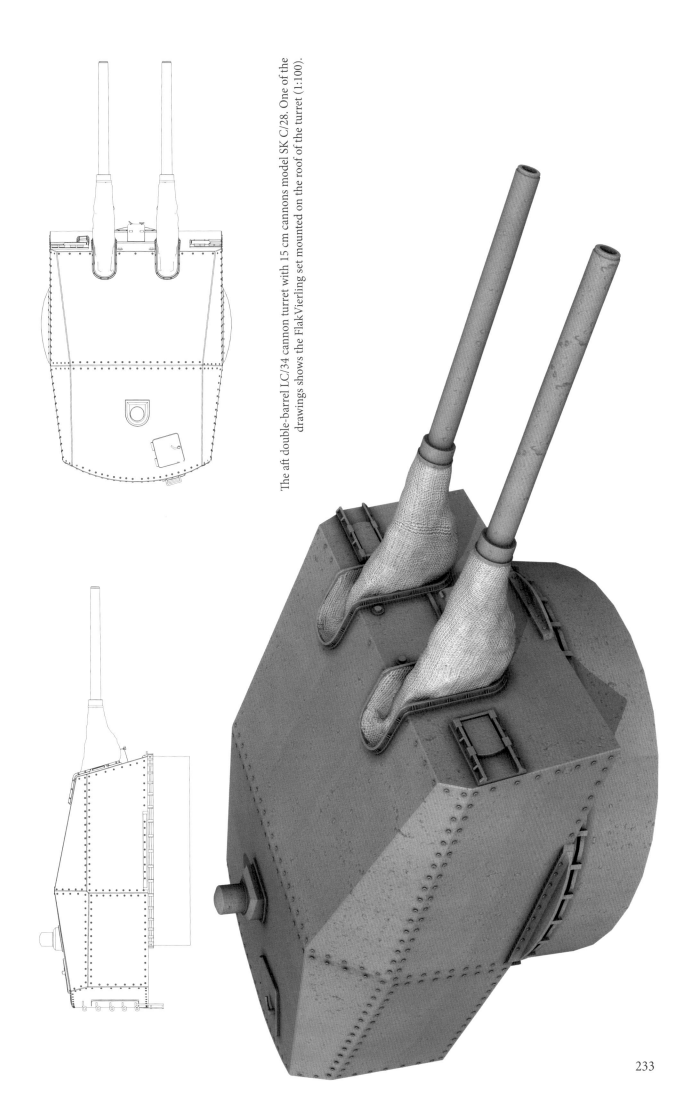

The aft double-barrel LC/34 cannon turret with 15 cm cannons model SK C/28. One of the drawings shows the FlakVierling set mounted on the roof of the turret (1:100).

233

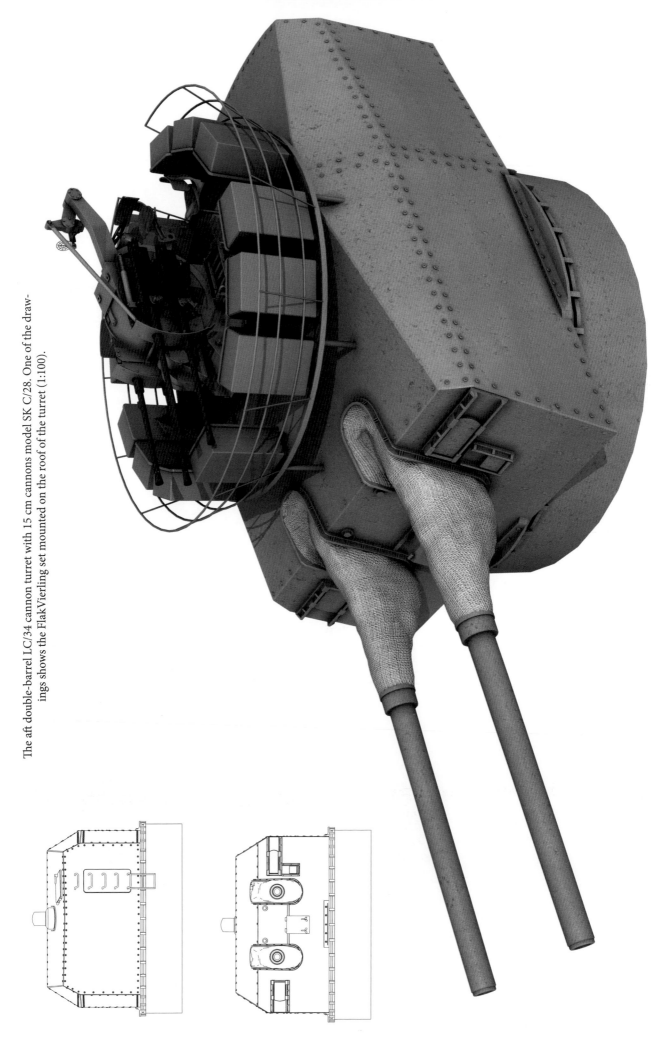

The aft double-barrel LC/34 cannon turret with 15 cm cannons model SK C/28. One of the drawings shows the FlakVierling set mounted on the roof of the turret (1:100).

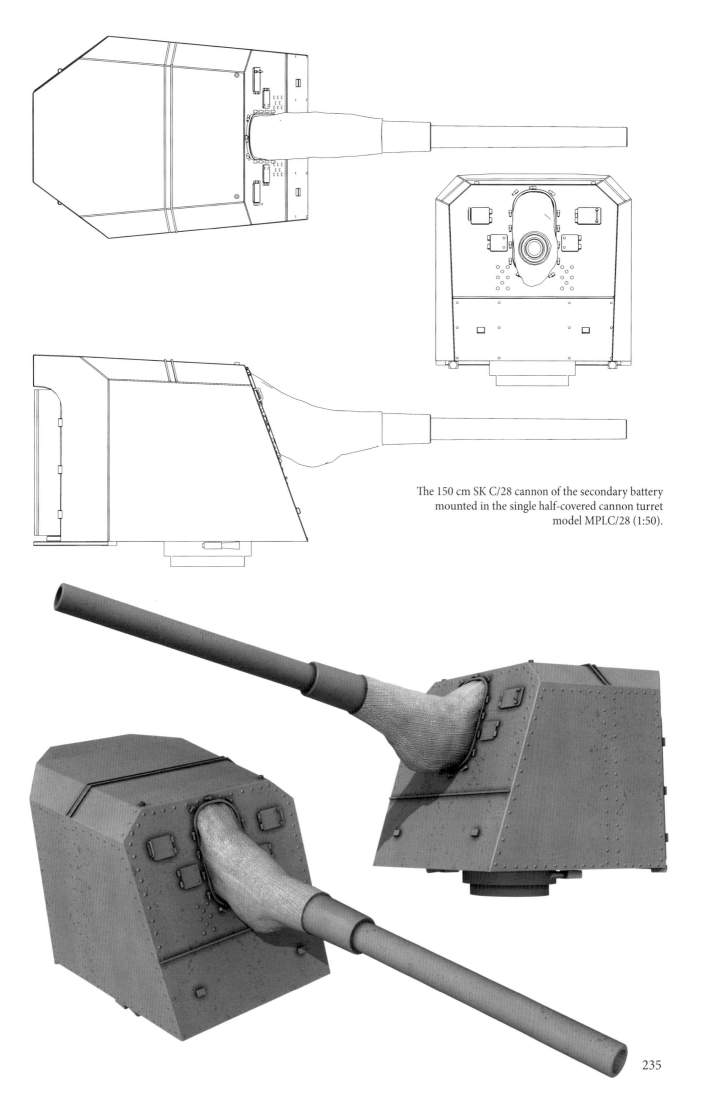

The 150 cm SK C/28 cannon of the secondary battery mounted in the single half-covered cannon turret model MPLC/28 (1:50).

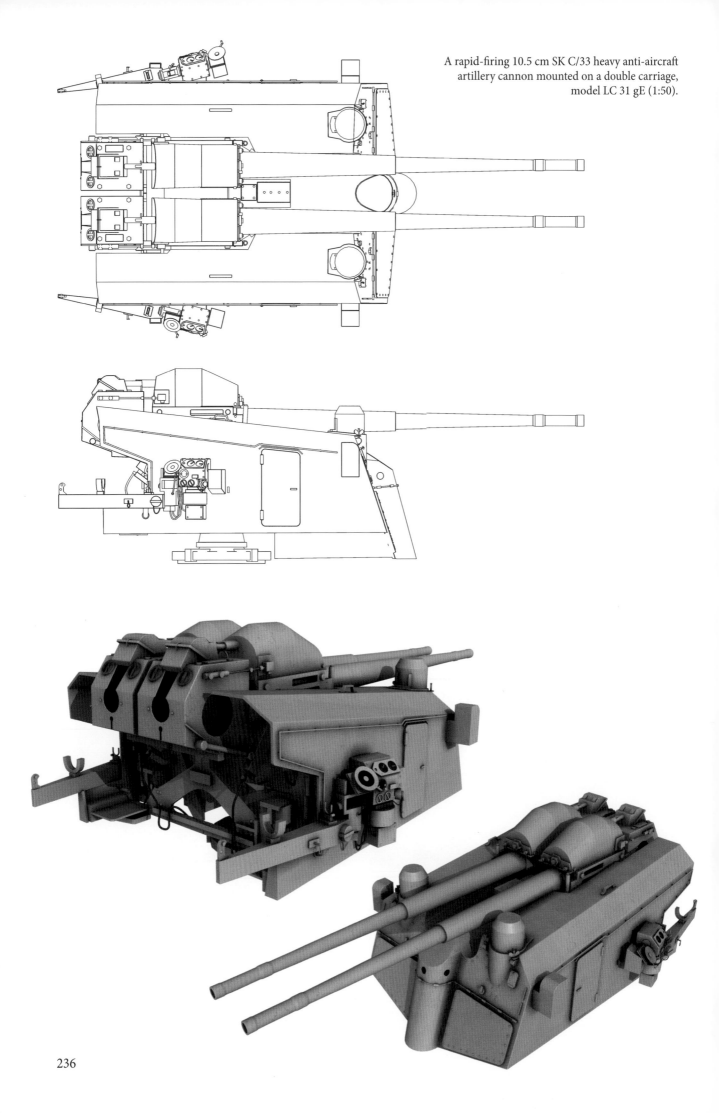

A rapid-firing 10.5 cm SK C/33 heavy anti-aircraft artillery cannon mounted on a double carriage, model LC 31 gE (1:50).

A rapid-firing 10.5 cm SK C/33 heavy anti-aircraft artillery cannon mounted on a double carriage, model LC 31 gE (1:50).

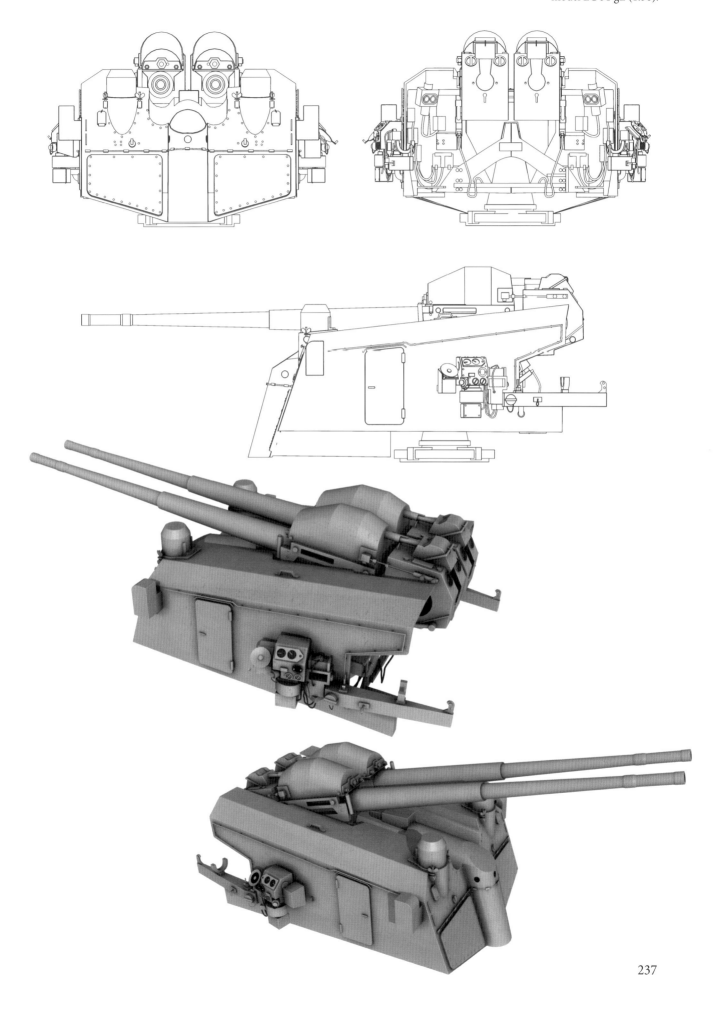

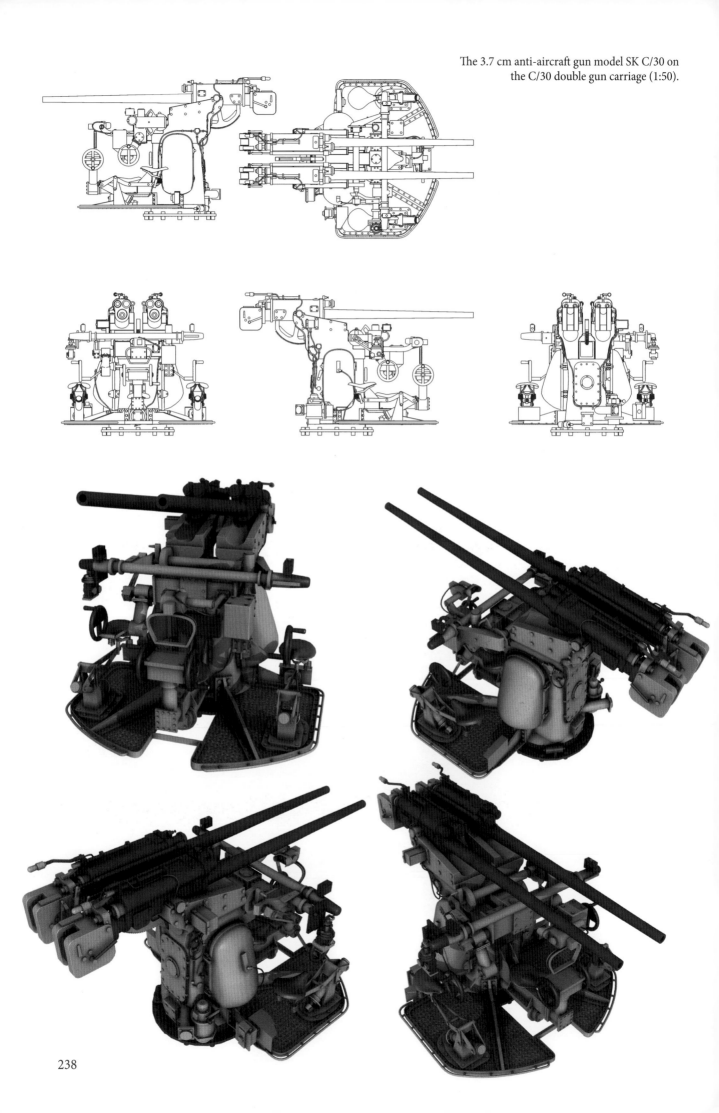

The 3.7 cm anti-aircraft gun model SK C/30 on the C/30 double gun carriage (1:50).

The 20 mm FlakVierling C35
AA gun (1:25).

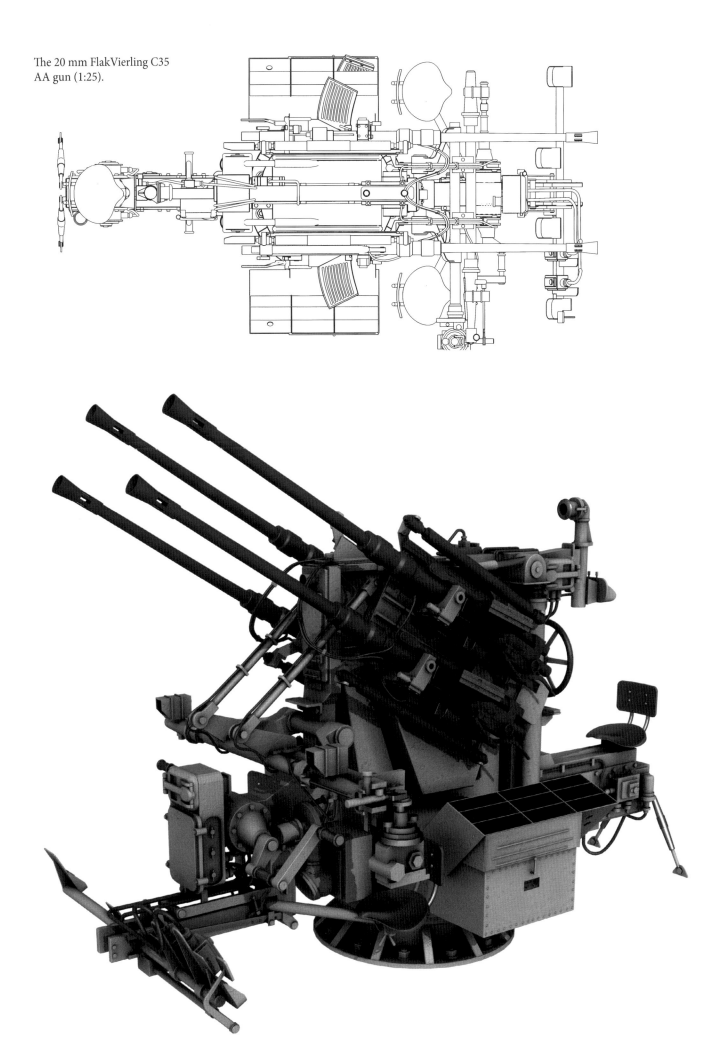

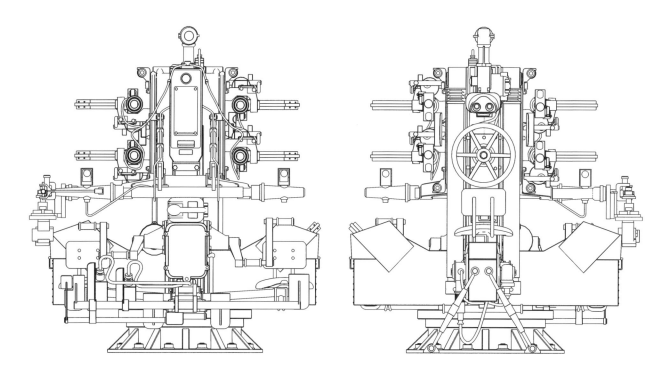

The 20 mm FlakVierling C35
AA gun (1:25).

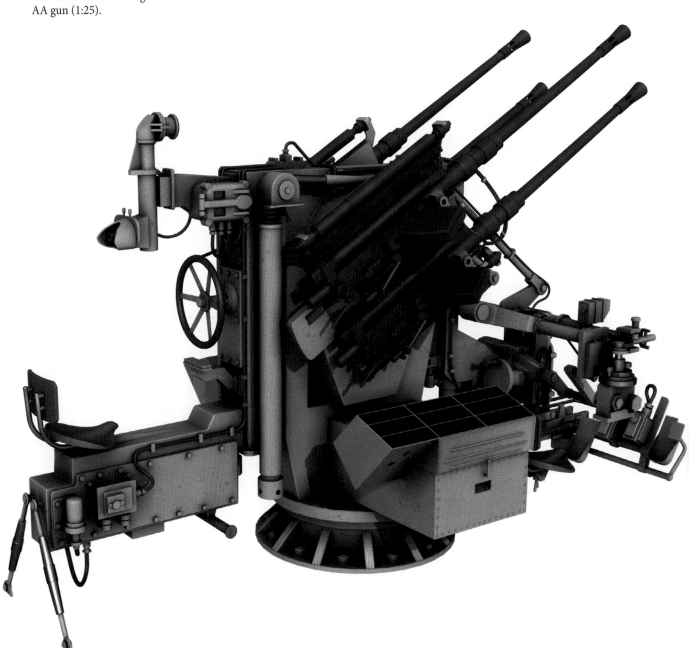

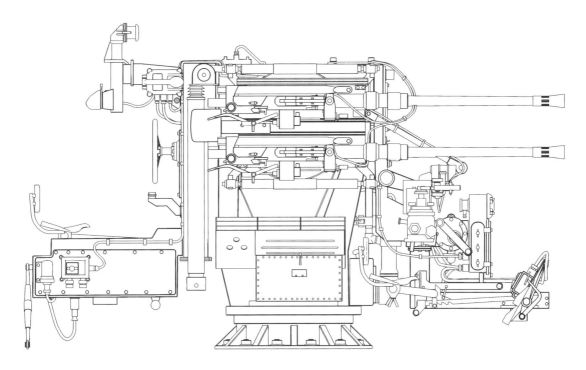

The 20 mm FlakVierling C35
AA gun (1:25).

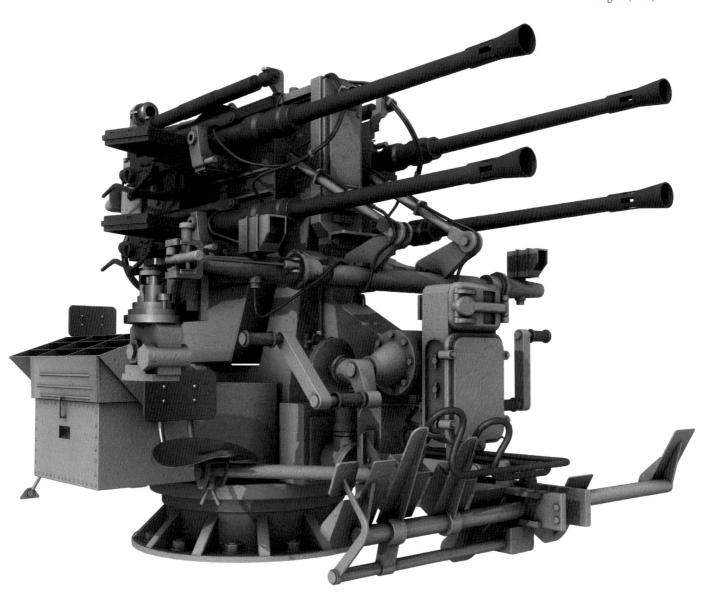

The 20 mm FlakVierling C35
AA gun (1:25).

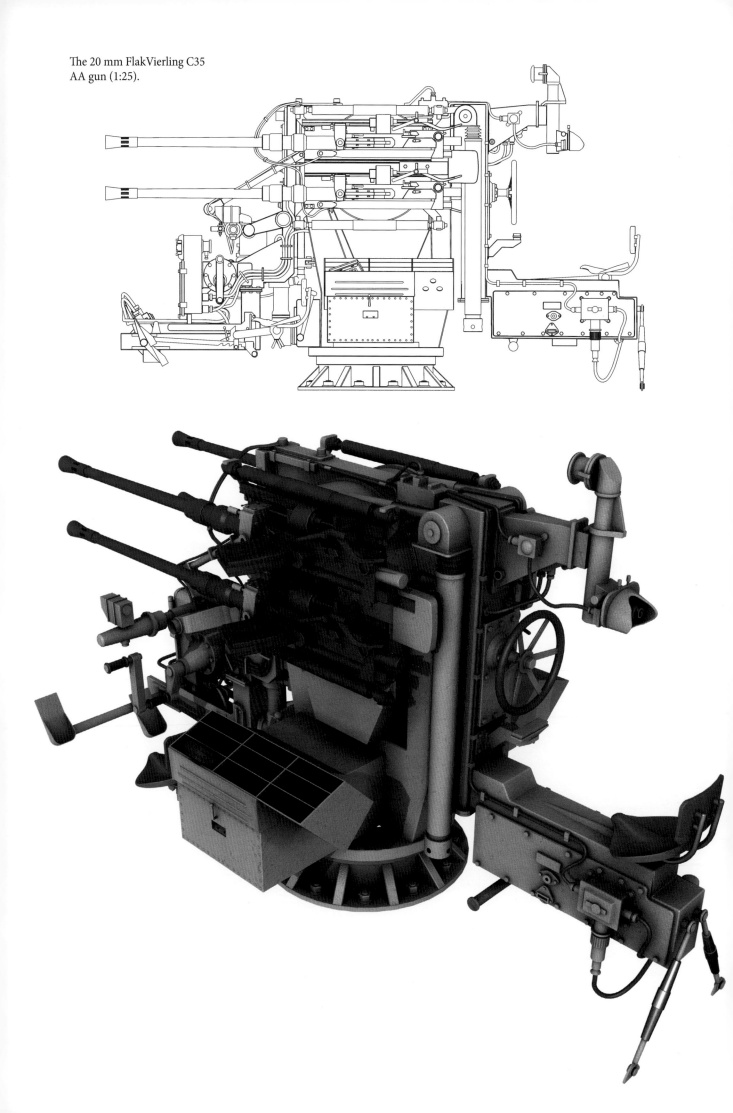

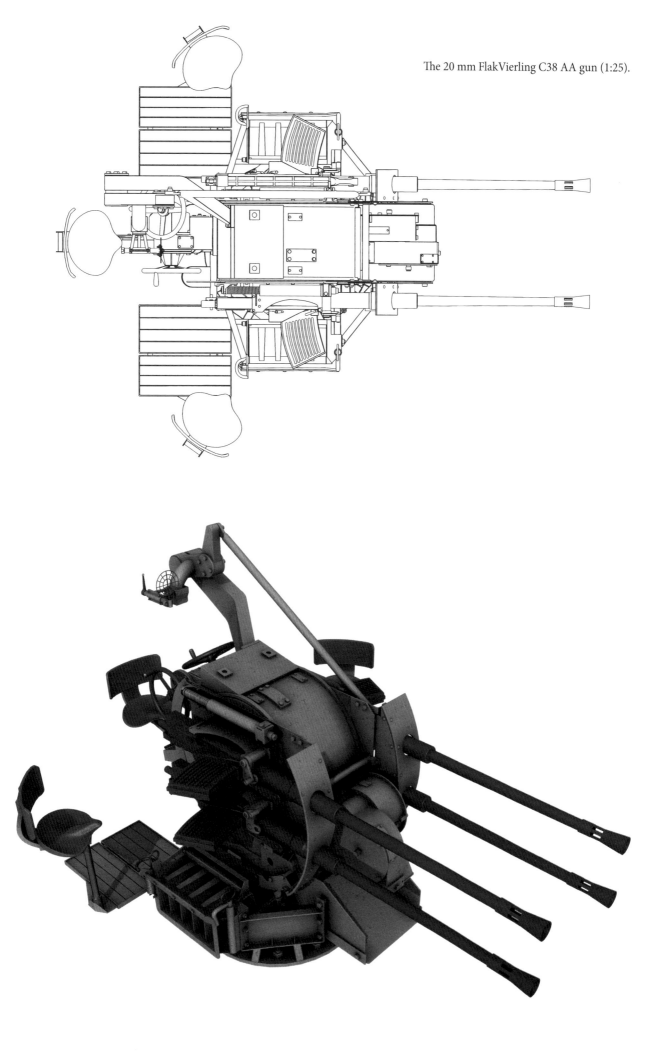

The 20 mm FlakVierling C38 AA gun (1:25).

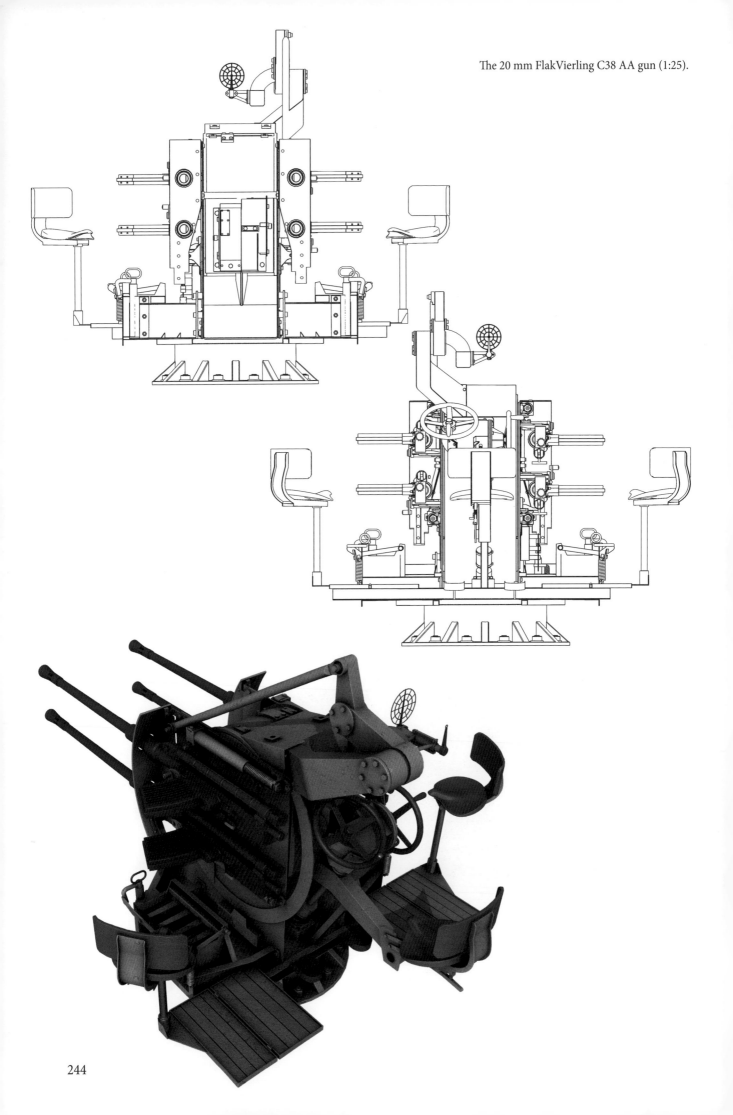

The 20 mm FlakVierling C38 AA gun (1:25).

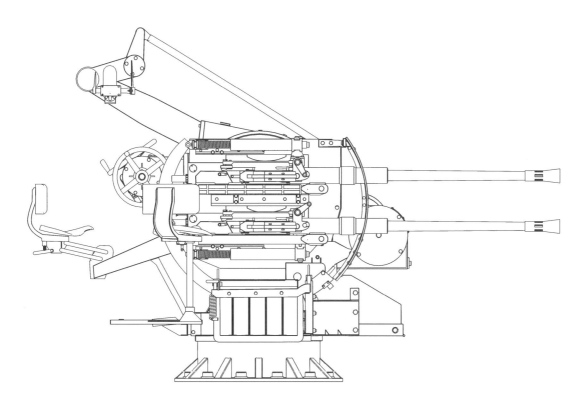

The 20 mm FlakVierling C38 AA gun (1:25).

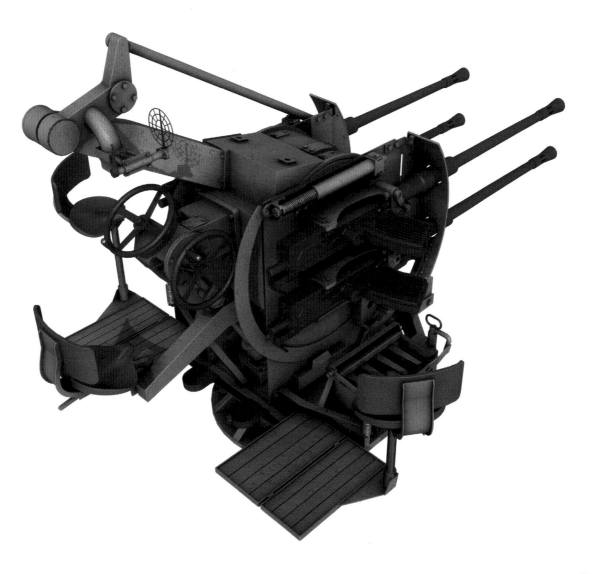

The 20 mm FlakVierling C38 AA gun (1:25).

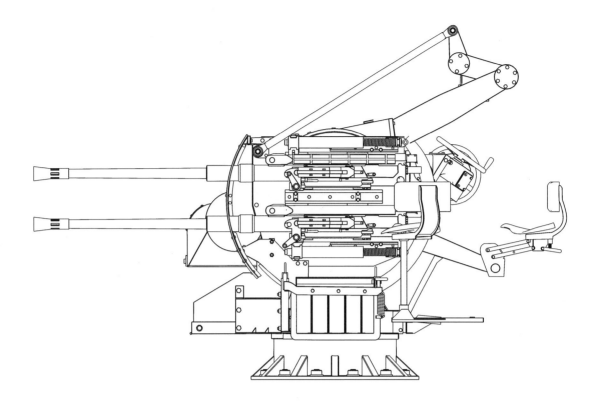

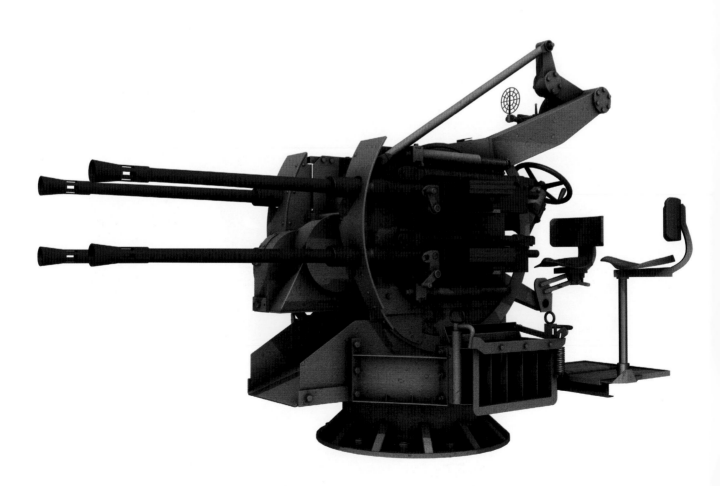

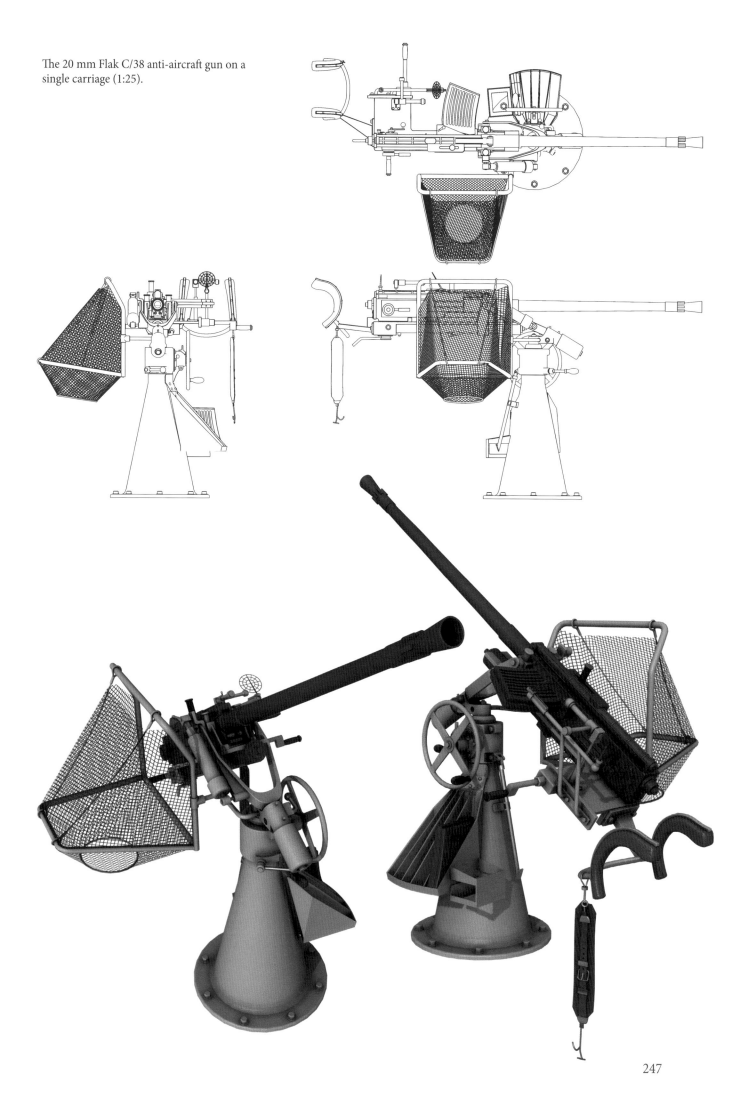

The 20 mm Flak C/38 anti-aircraft gun on a single carriage (1:25).

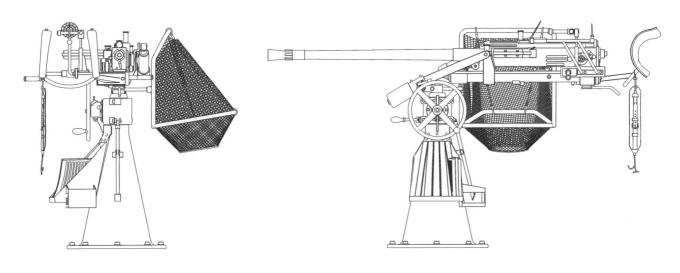

The 20 mm Flak C/38 anti-aircraft gun on a
single carriage (1:25).

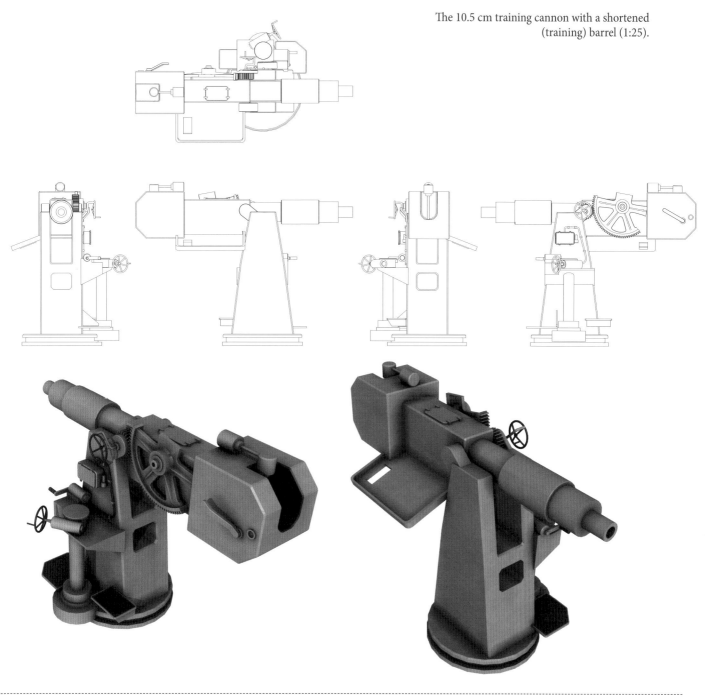

The 10.5 cm training cannon with a shortened (training) barrel (1:25).

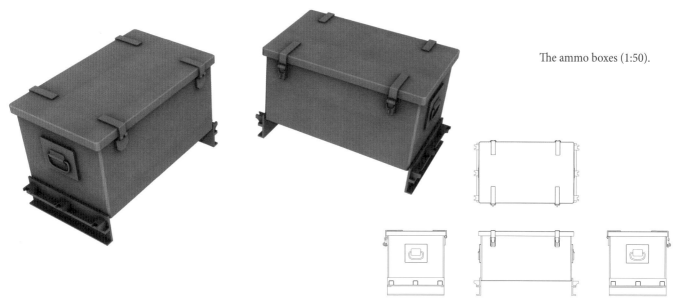

The ammo boxes (1:50).

The three-tube 533 mm torpedo launcher (1:50).

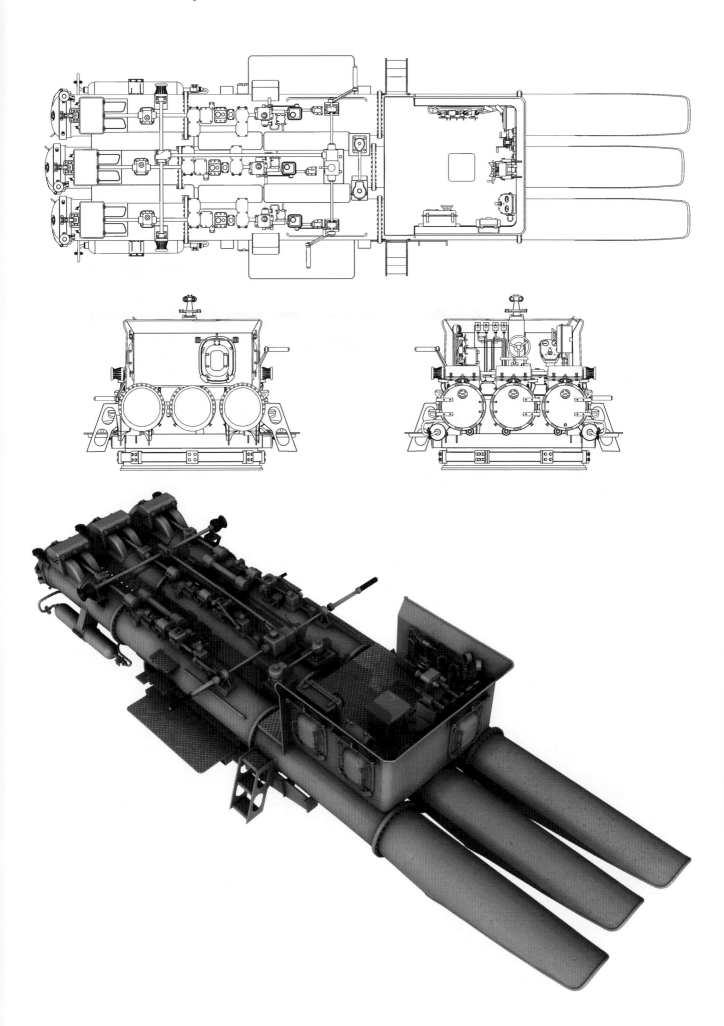

The three-tube 533 mm torpedo launcher (version with a cover on the front of the launcher) (1:50).

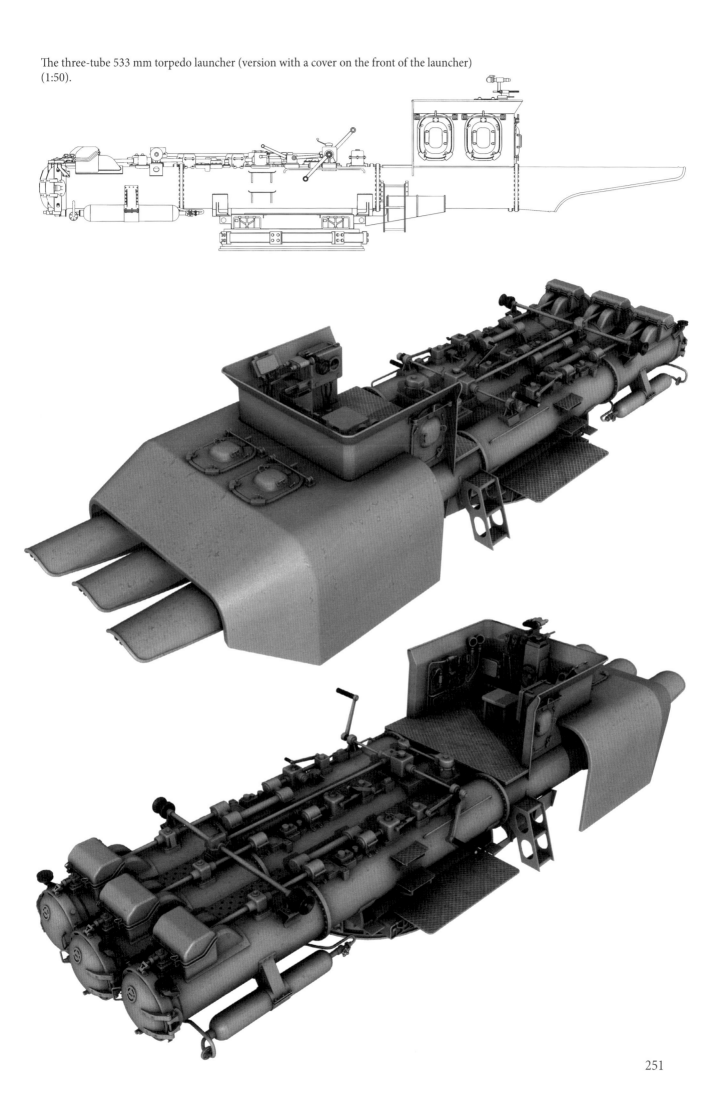

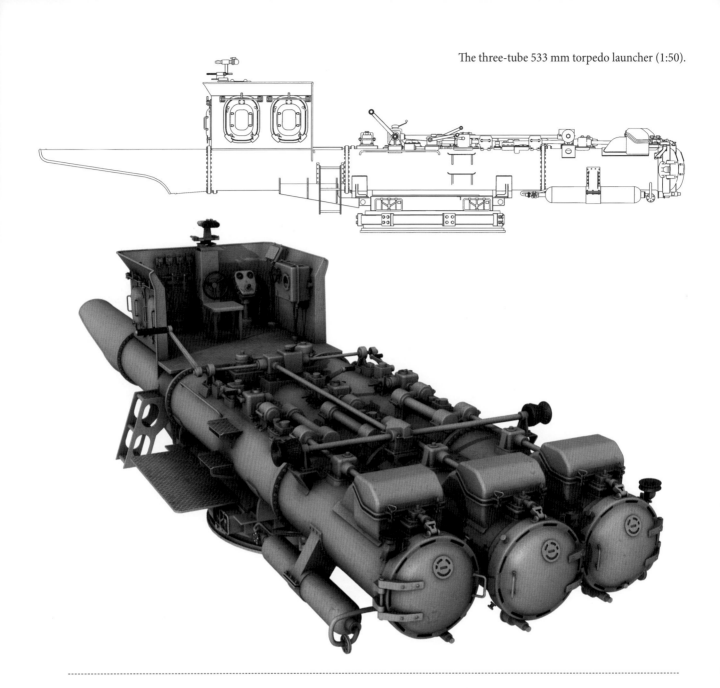

The three-tube 533 mm torpedo launcher (1:50).

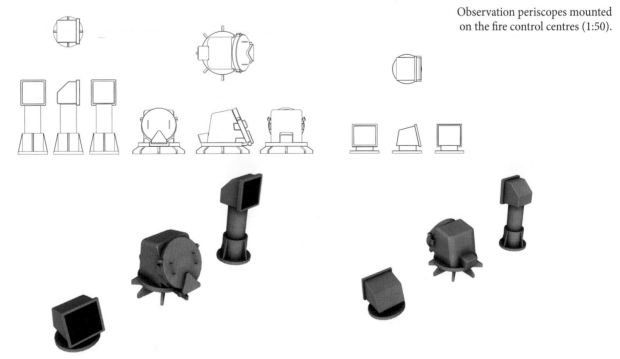

Observation periscopes mounted on the fire control centres (1:50).

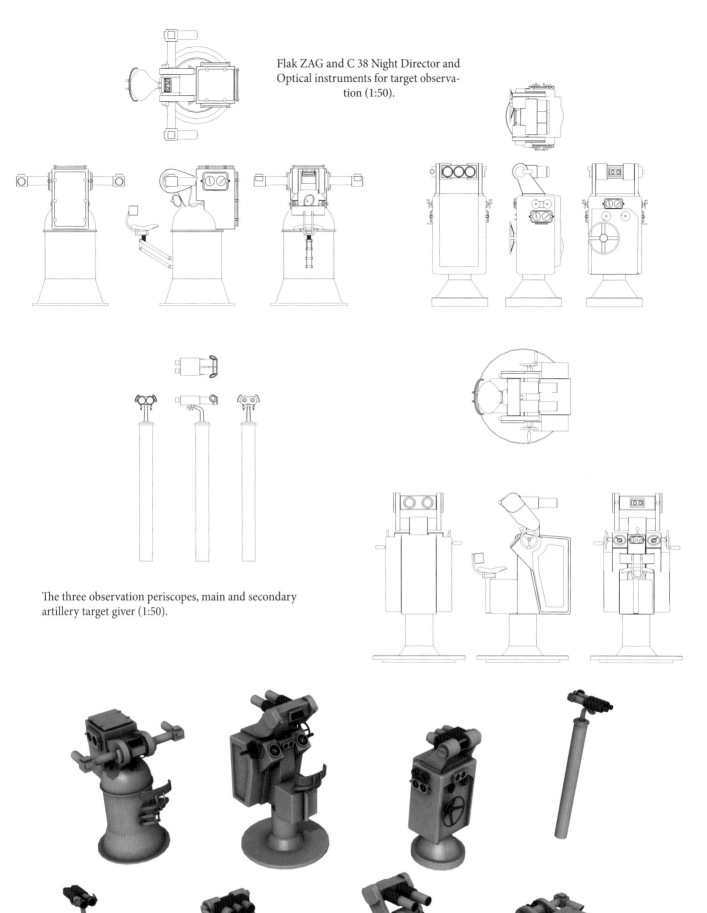

Flak ZAG and C 38 Night Director and Optical instruments for target observation (1:50).

The three observation periscopes, main and secondary artillery target giver (1:50).

The bow flag pole (Jack Staff) (1:100).

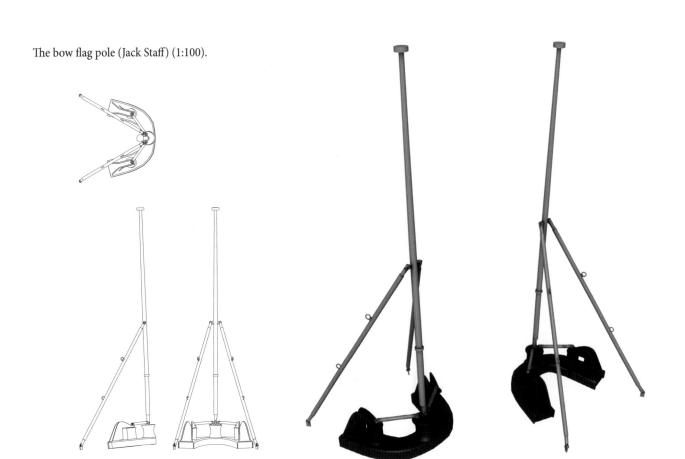

The aft flag pole (Flag Staff) (1:100).

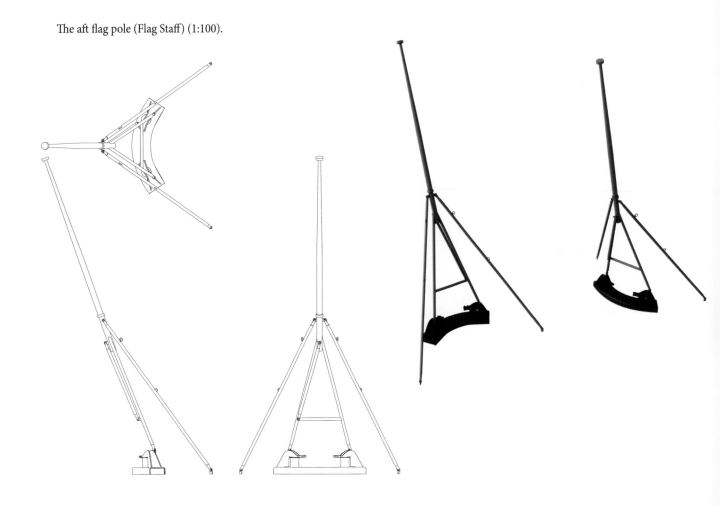

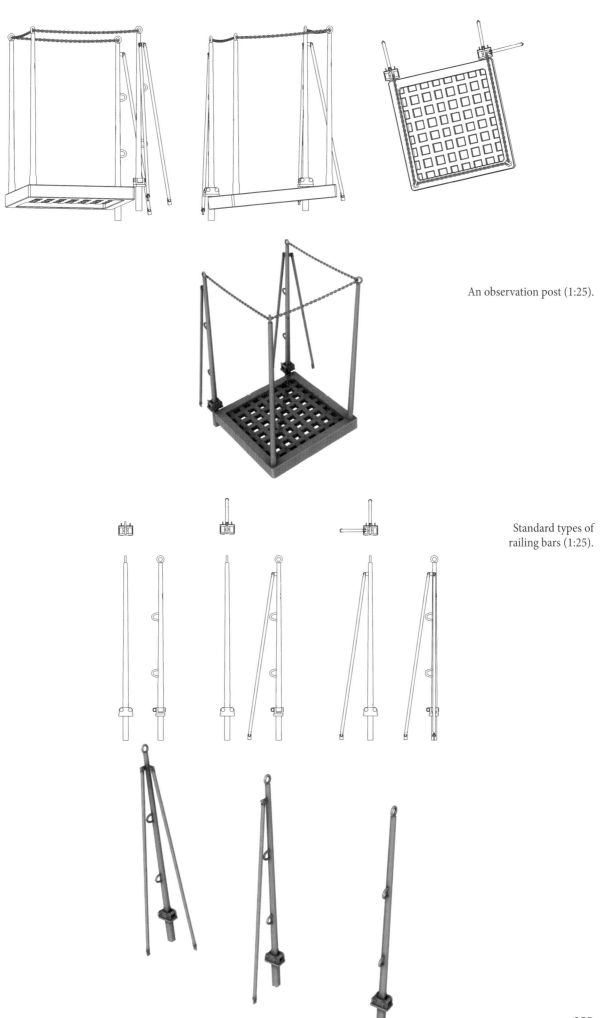

An observation post (1:25).

Standard types of
railing bars (1:25).

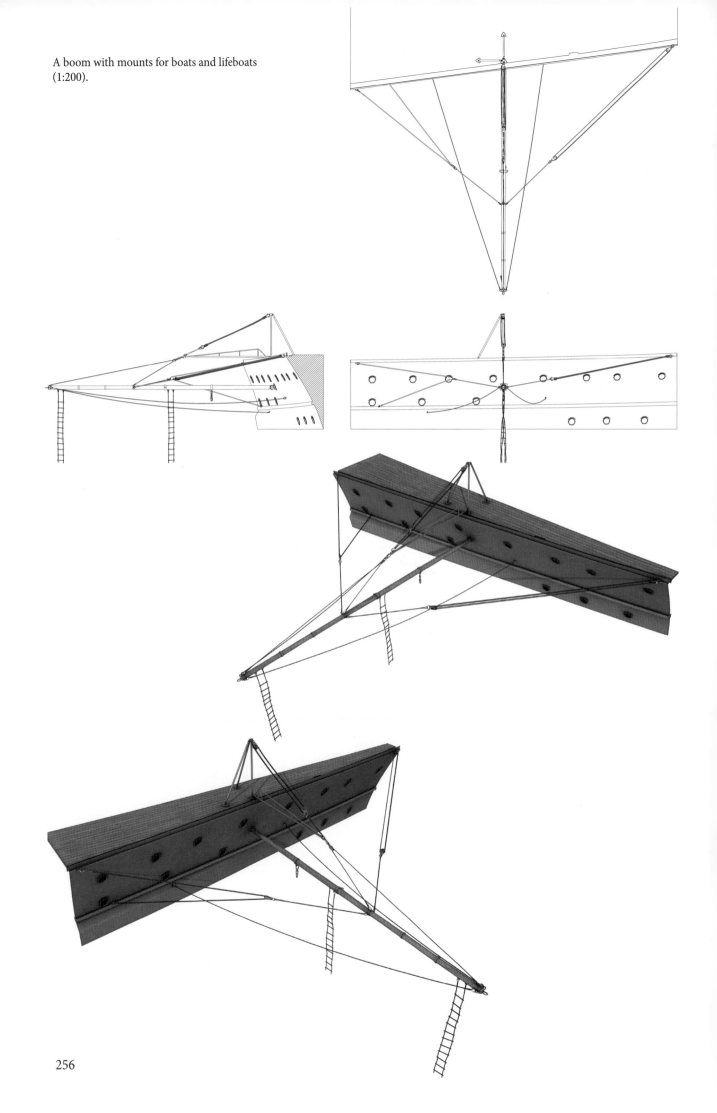

A boom with mounts for boats and lifeboats
(1:200).

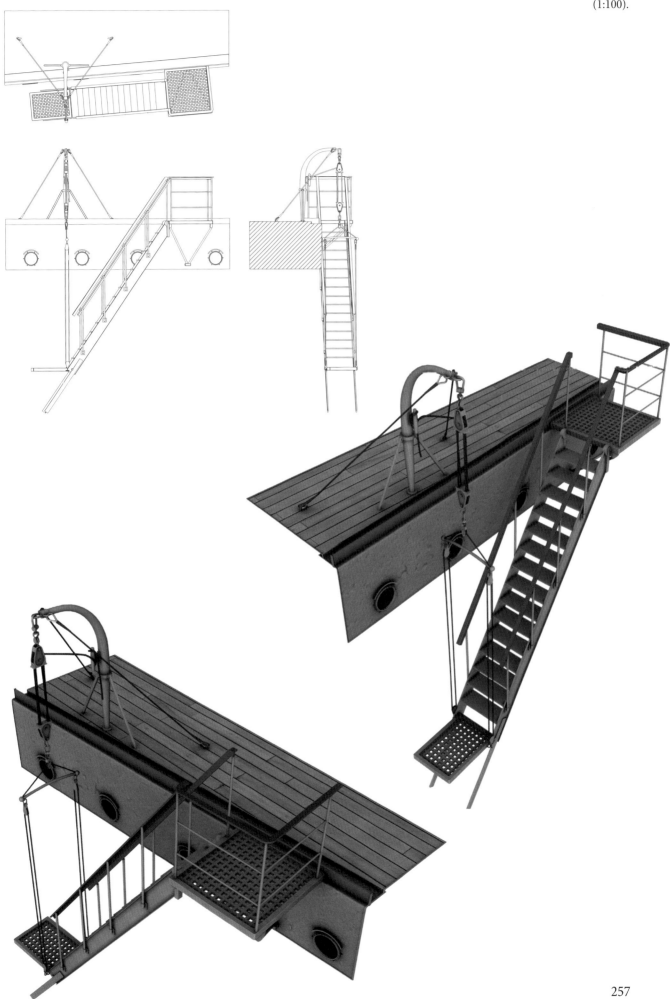

The descent gangway, davit and the way it was fastened (1:100).

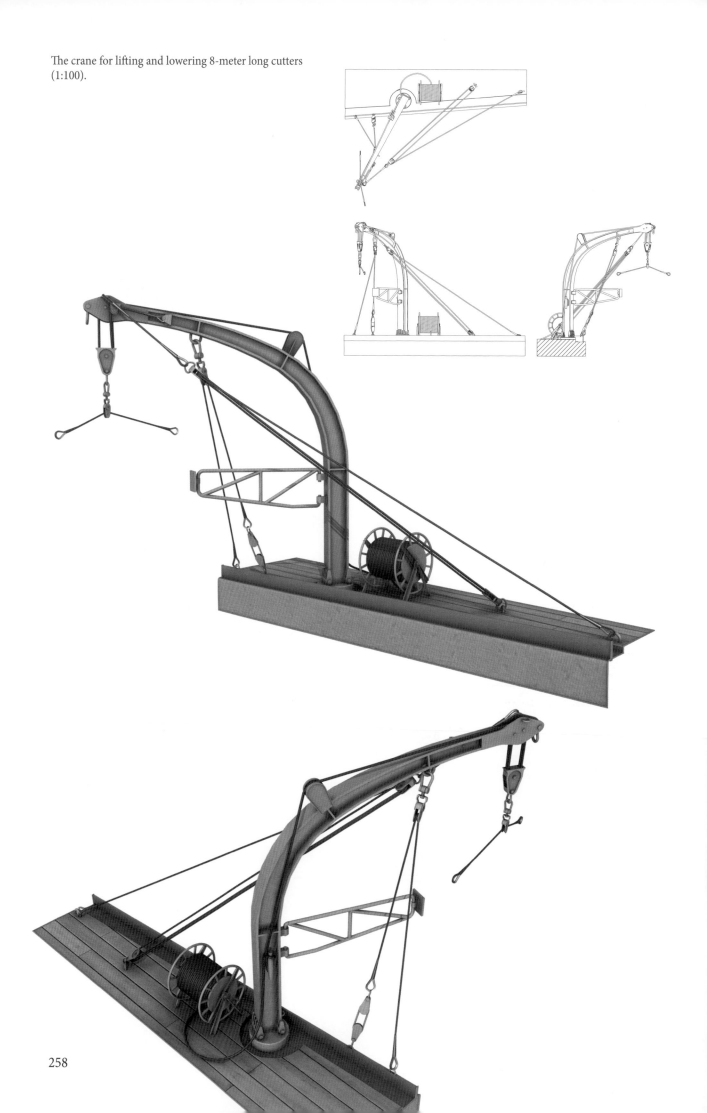

The crane for lifting and lowering 8-meter long cutters (1:100).

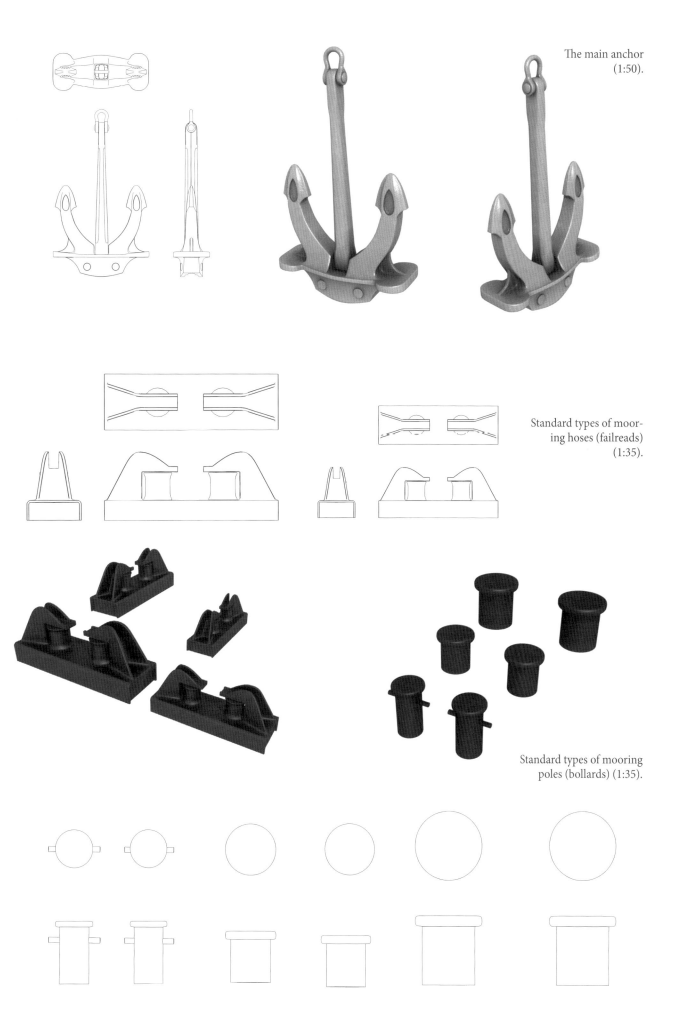

The main anchor
(1:50).

Standard types of mooring hoses (failreads)
(1:35).

Standard types of mooring
poles (bollards) (1:35).

259

The aft capstan (1:50).

The bow capstan (1:50).

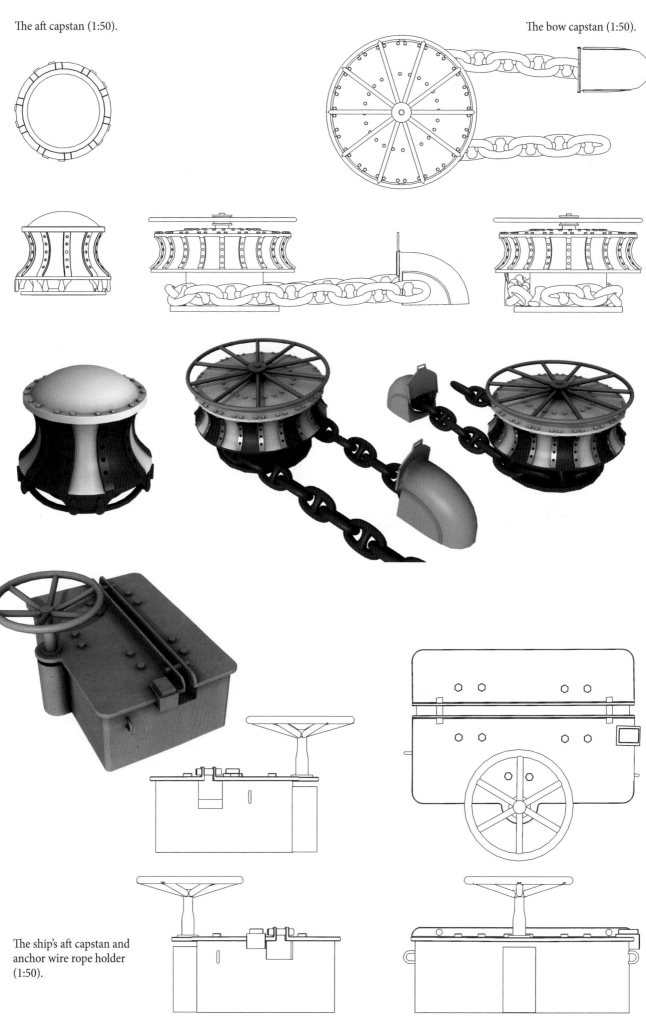

The ship's aft capstan and
anchor wire rope holder
(1:50).

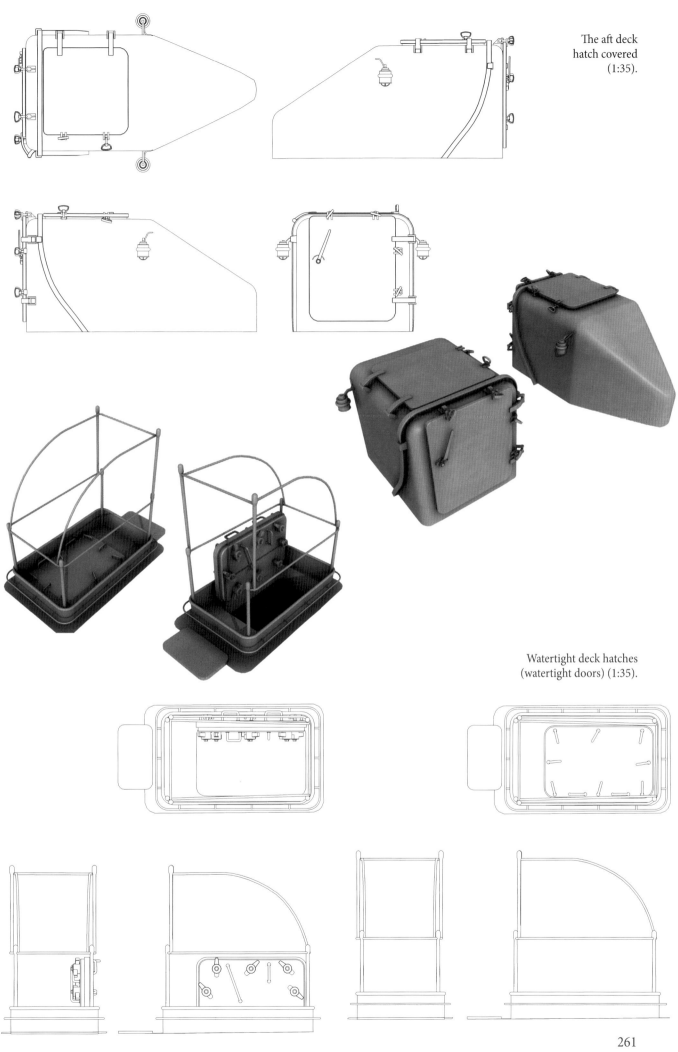

The aft deck
hatch covered
(1:35).

Watertight deck hatches
(watertight doors) (1:35).

261

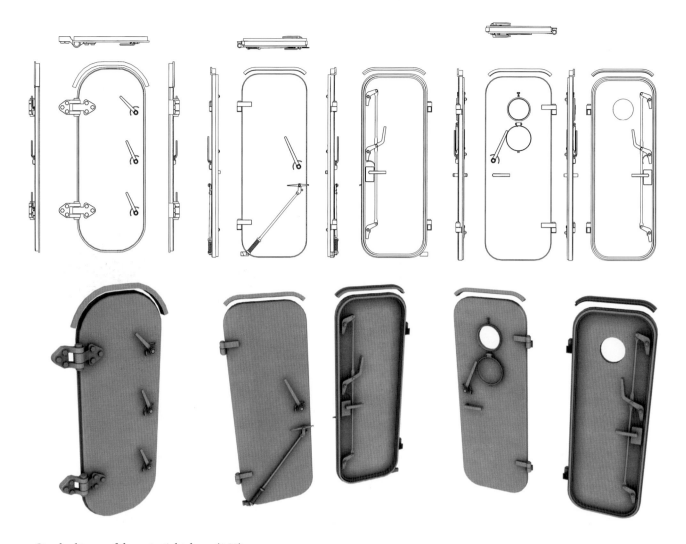

Standard types of the watertight doors (1:35).
The watertight doors open.
The watertight doors closed.

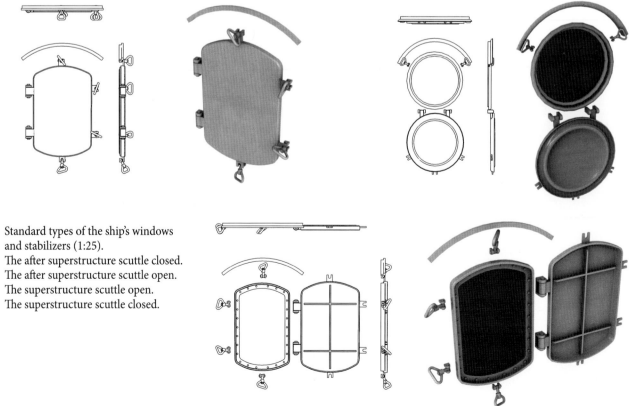

Standard types of the ship's windows
and stabilizers (1:25).
The after superstructure scuttle closed.
The after superstructure scuttle open.
The superstructure scuttle open.
The superstructure scuttle closed.

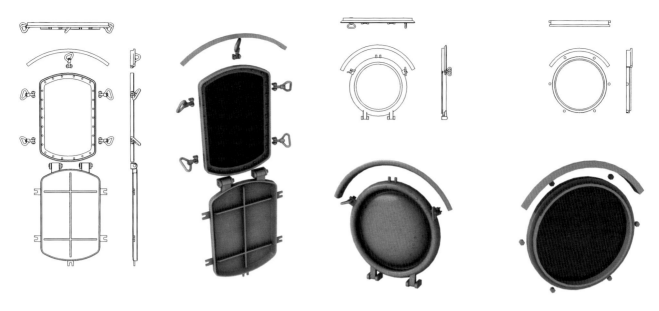

The after superstructure scuttle closed.

Standard types of skylights (1:25).

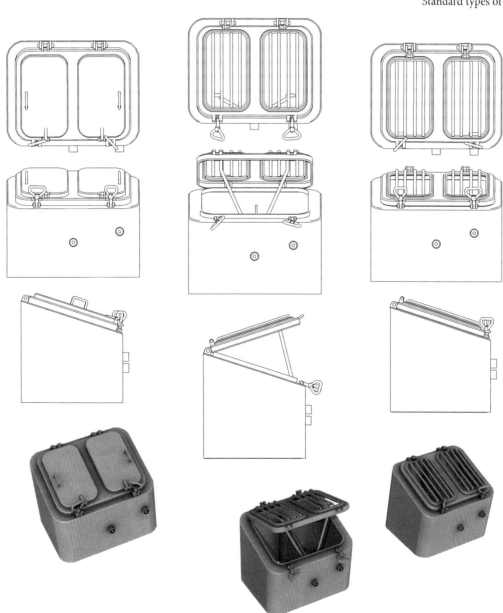

263

Cannon barrel pods
(1:35).

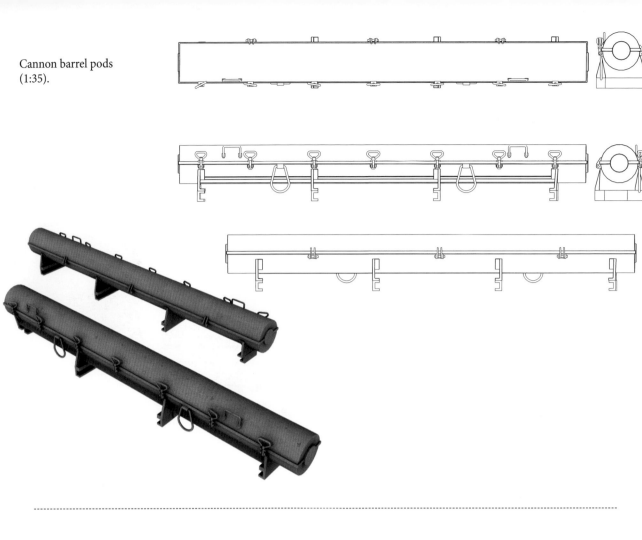

Standard types of handheld toolboxes (1:35).

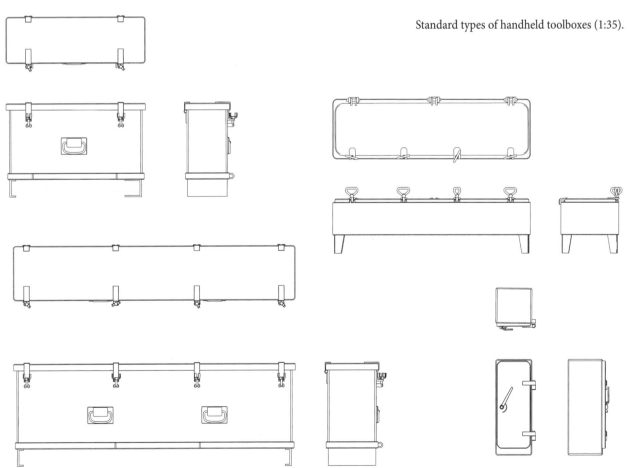

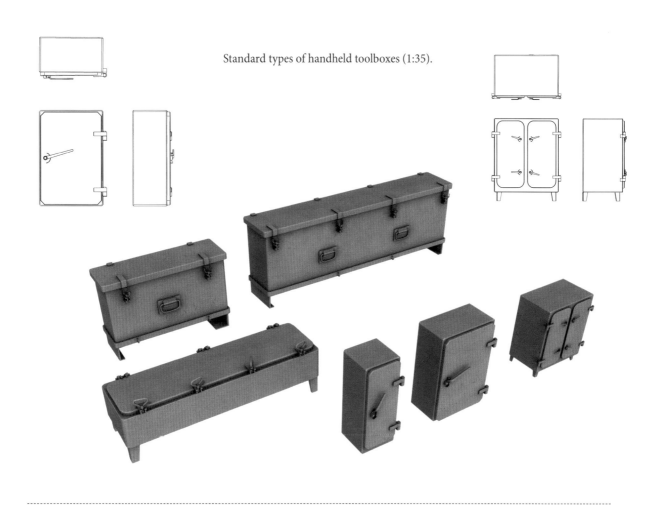

Standard types of handheld toolboxes (1:35).

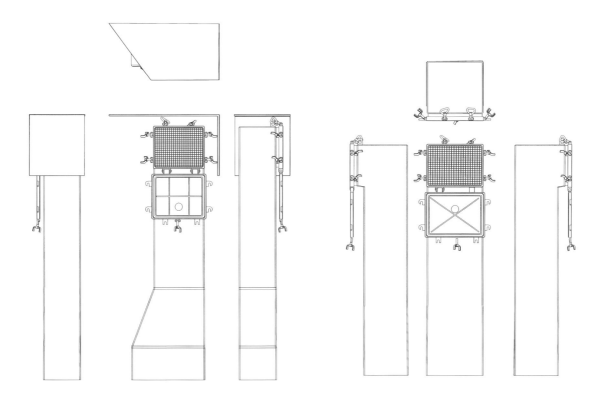

Standard types of diffusers and ventilation shafts (1:35).

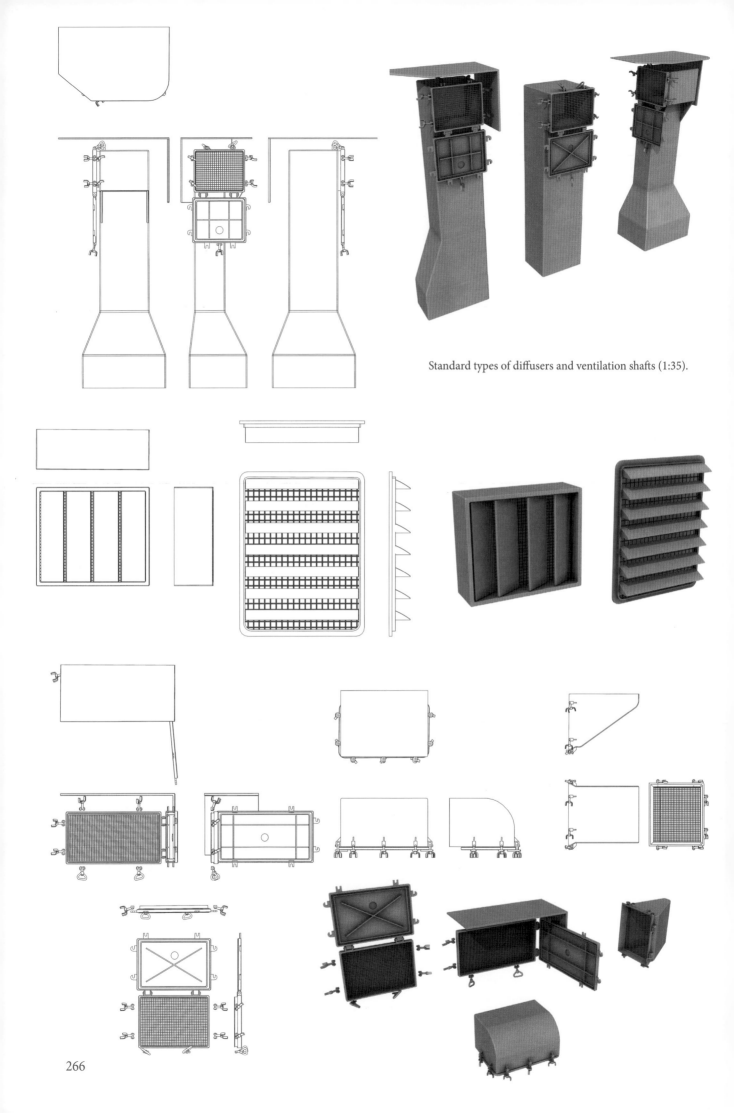

Standard types of diffusers and ventilation shafts (1:35).

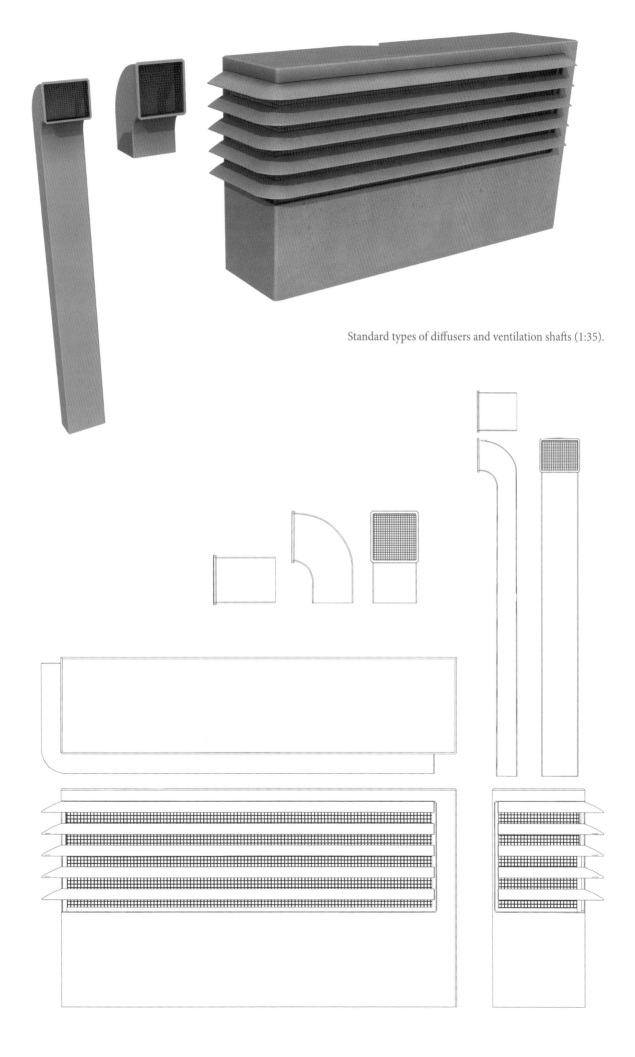

Standard types of diffusers and ventilation shafts (1:35).

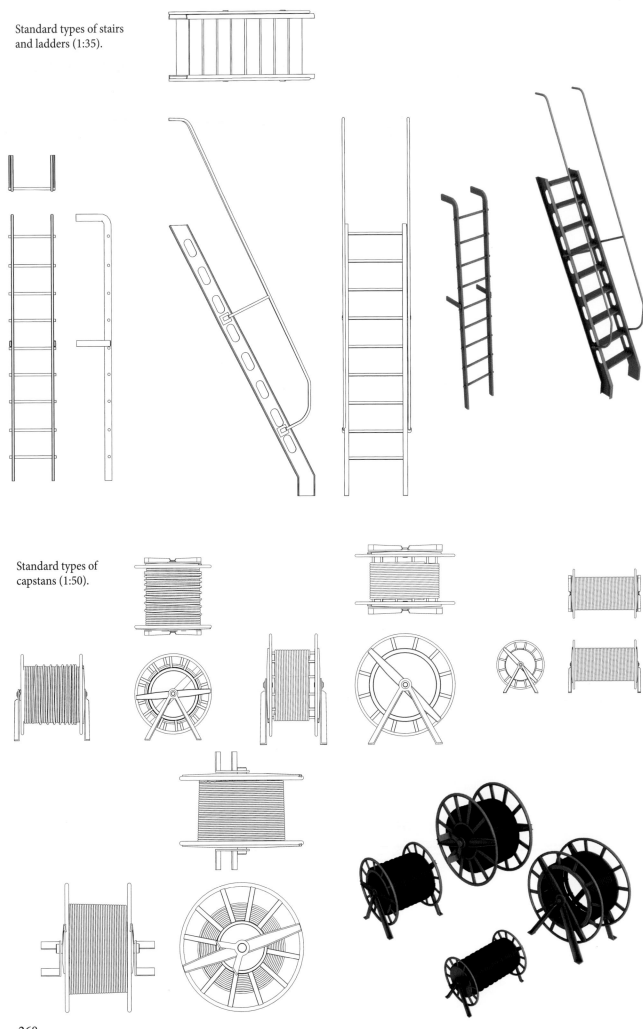

Standard types of stairs and ladders (1:35).

Standard types of capstans (1:50).

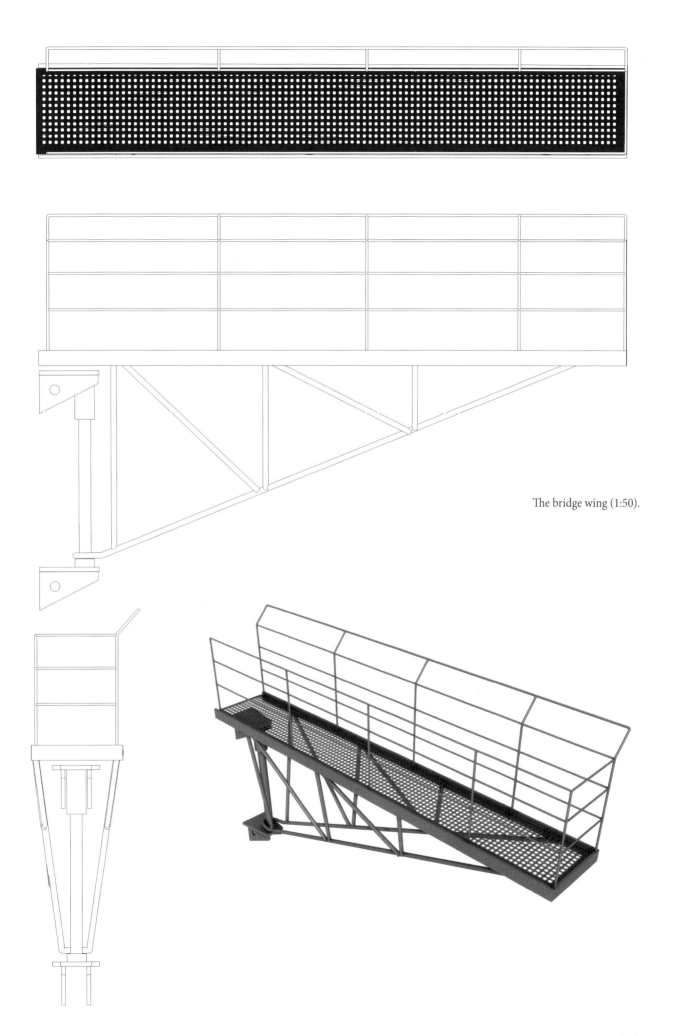

The bridge wing (1:50).

The paravane (1:25).

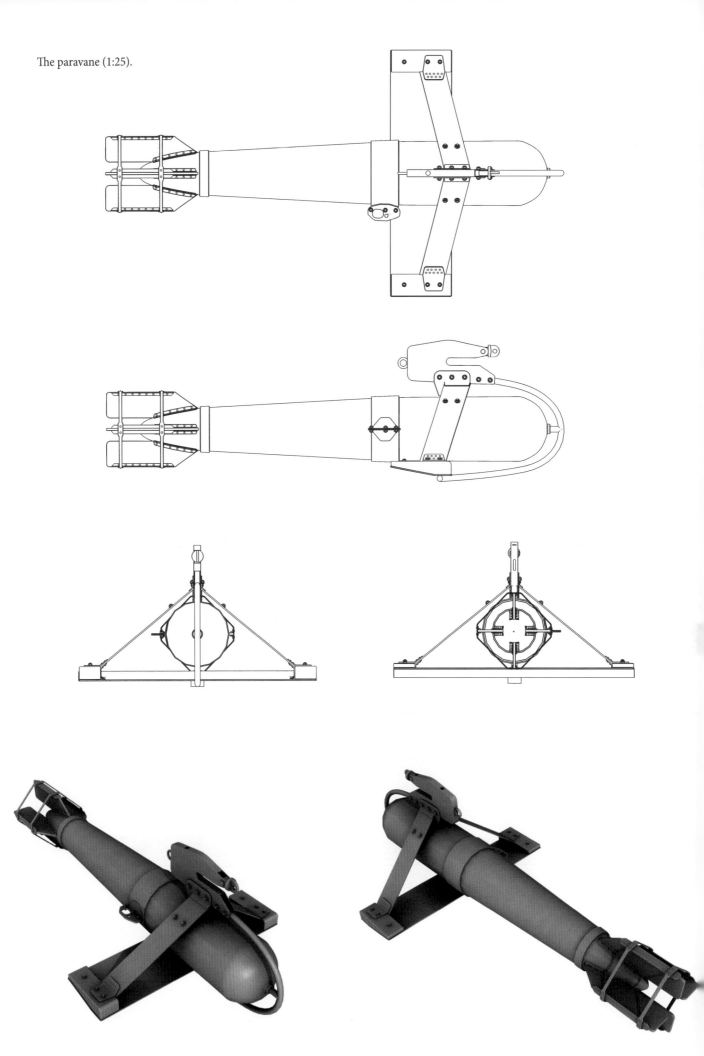

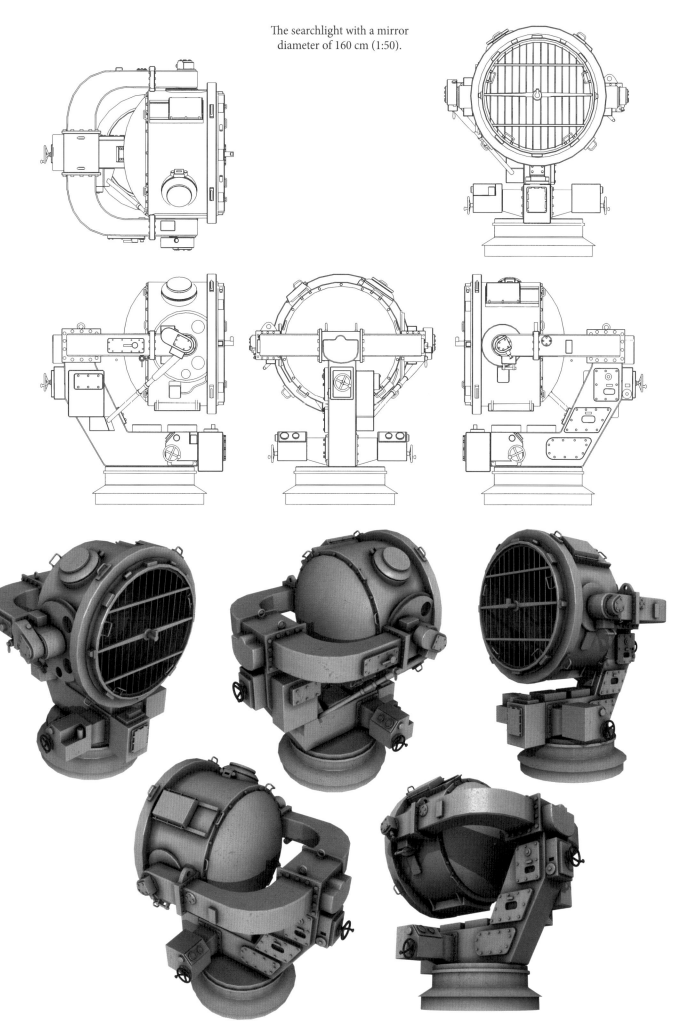

The searchlight with a mirror diameter of 160 cm (1:50).

271

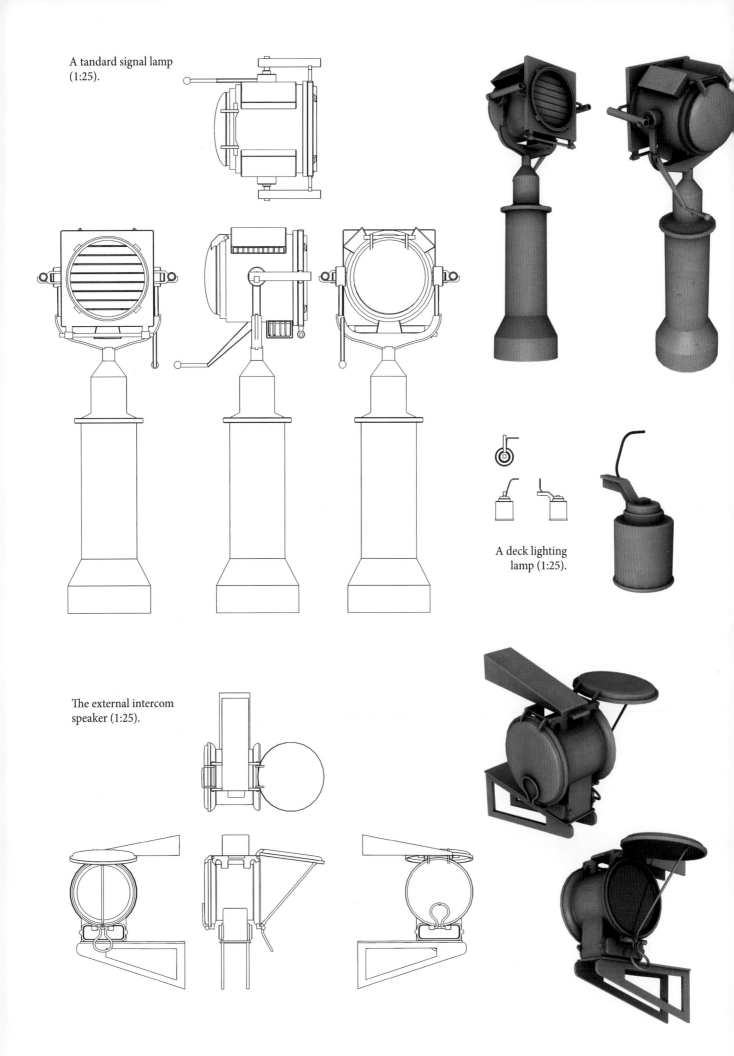

A tandard signal lamp
(1:25).

A deck lighting
lamp (1:25).

The external intercom
speaker (1:25).

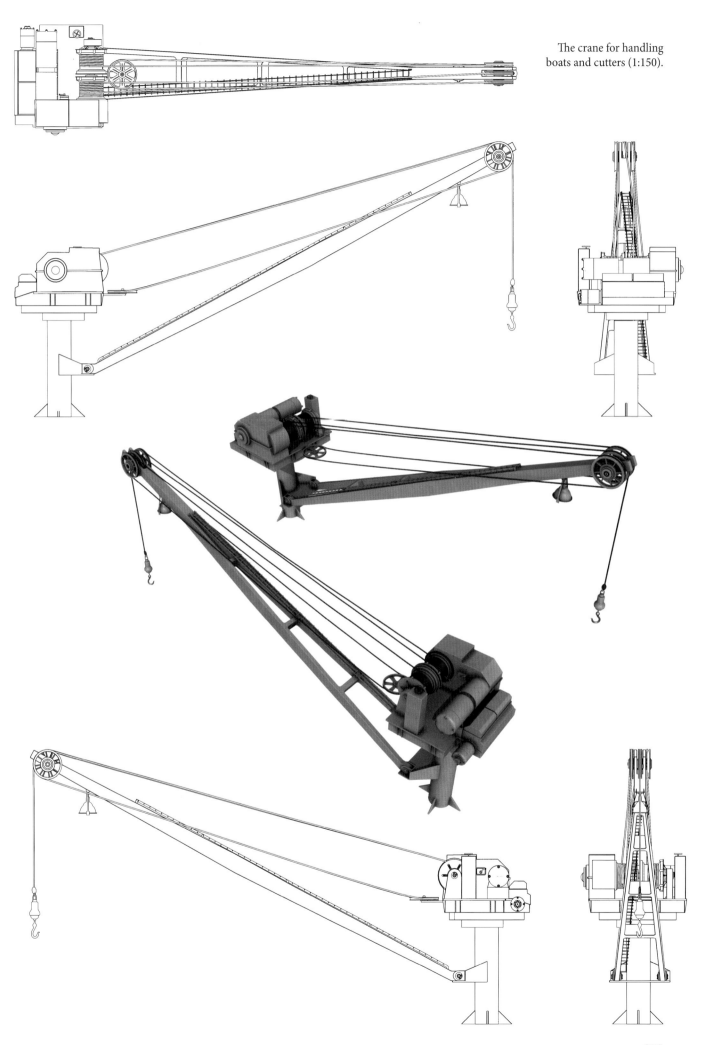

The crane for handling boats and cutters (1:150).

A 11 m communication boat (launch) (1:100).

The 9,2 Captain's Gig (1:100).

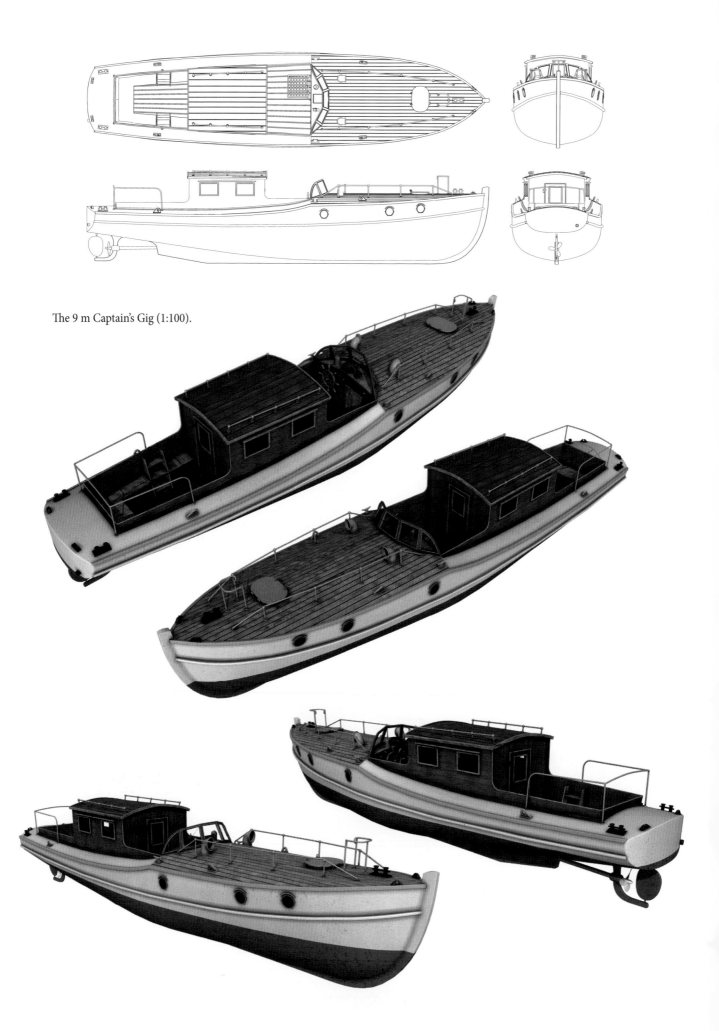

The 9 m Captain's Gig (1:100).

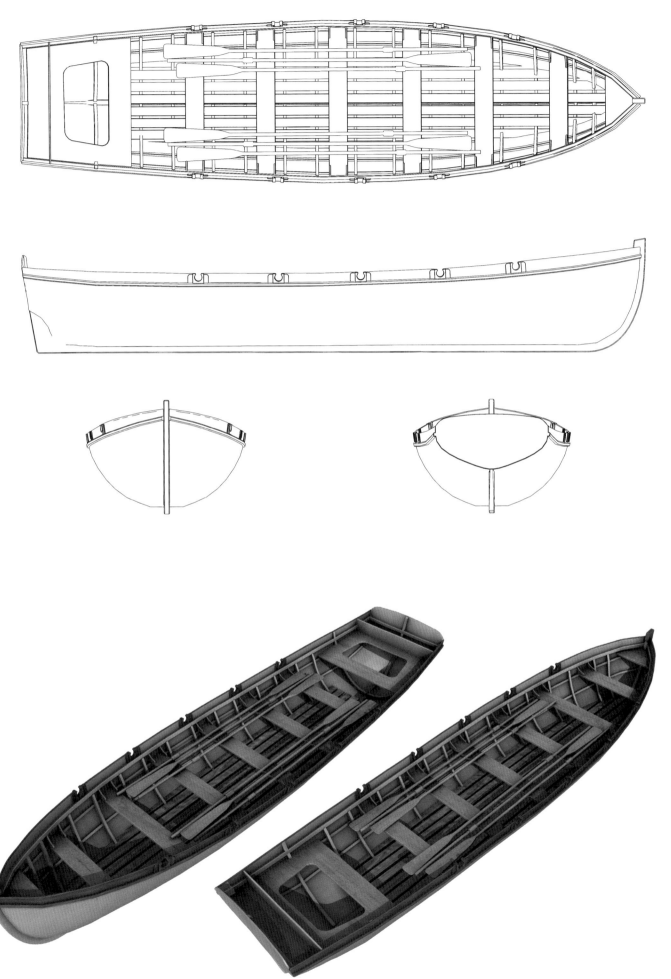

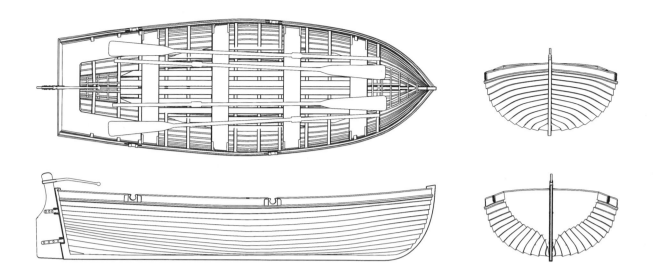

The 5-m-long lifeboat (1:50).

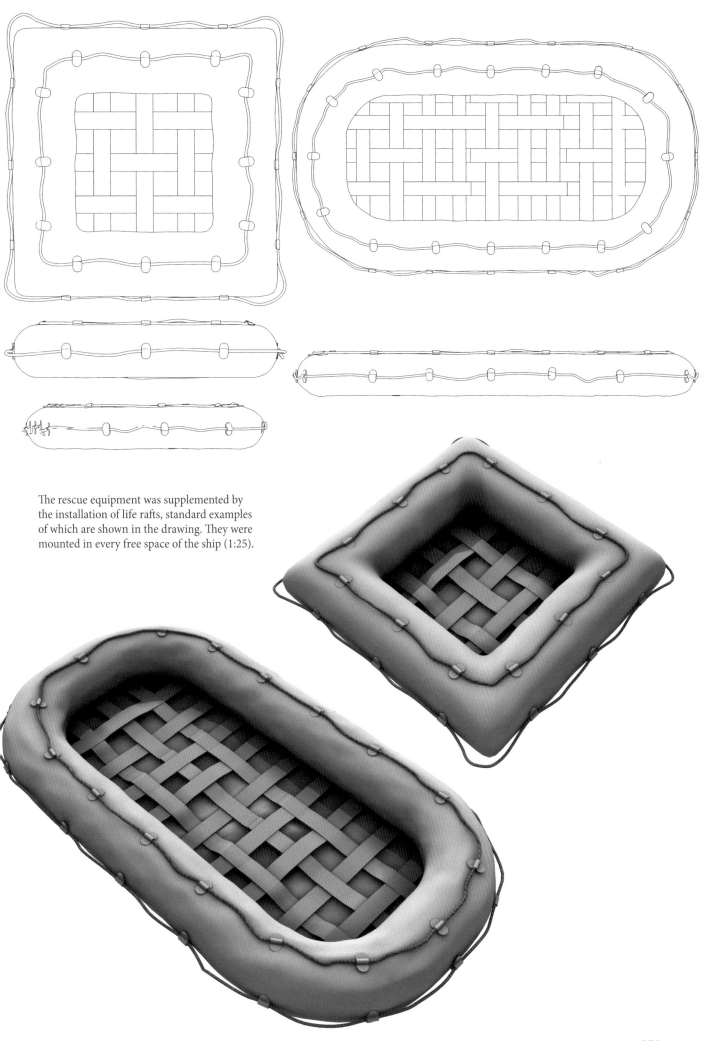

The rescue equipment was supplemented by the installation of life rafts, standard examples of which are shown in the drawing. They were mounted in every free space of the ship (1:25).

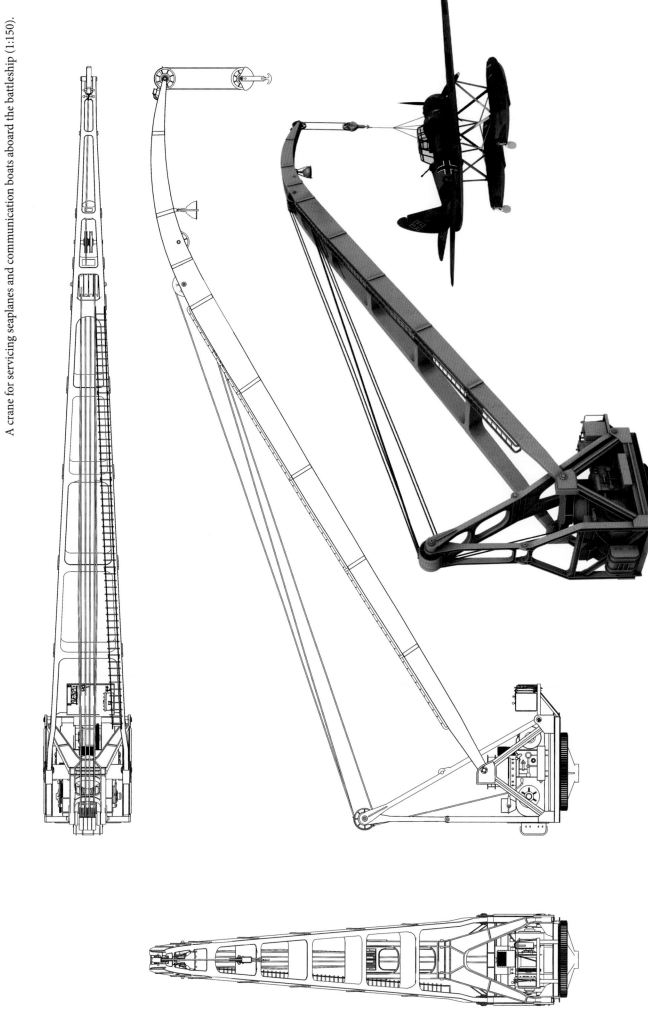

A crane for servicing seaplanes and communication boats aboard the battleship (1:150).

A crane for servicing seaplanes and communication boats aboard the battleship (1:150).

The Arado Ar 196 - A2 1.BordFlGr196 seaplane designated (T3+NH) Wrk.N. 1960040 that, among others, was included in the battleship's equipment (1:100).

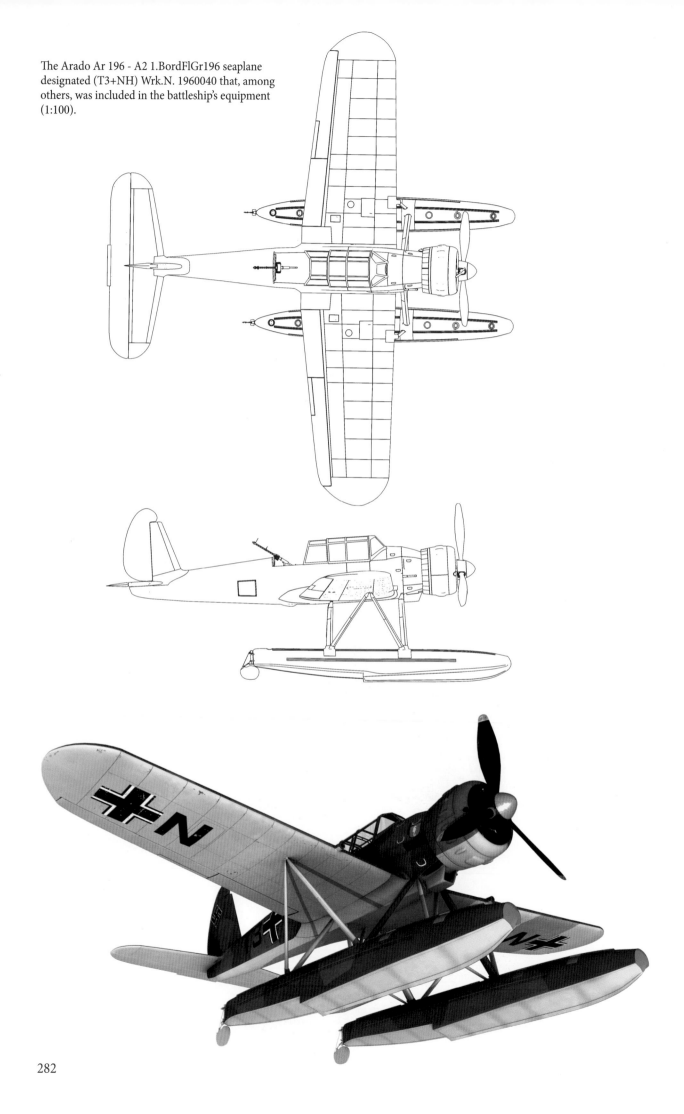

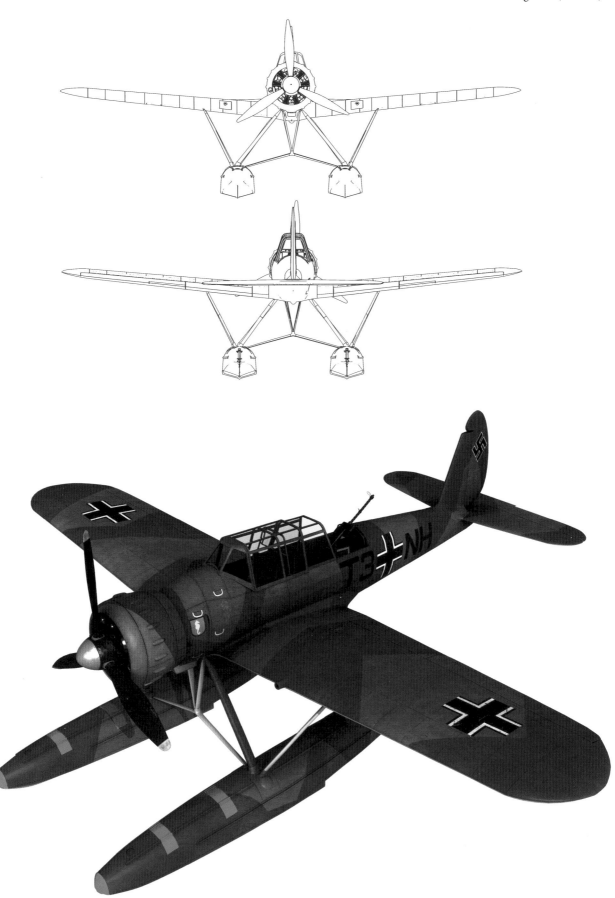

The Arado Ar 196 in geometric camouflage painting. On the side, there is the emblem of the group – a white waterhorse on a blue shield surrounded by a border. It was designated (T3+NH).

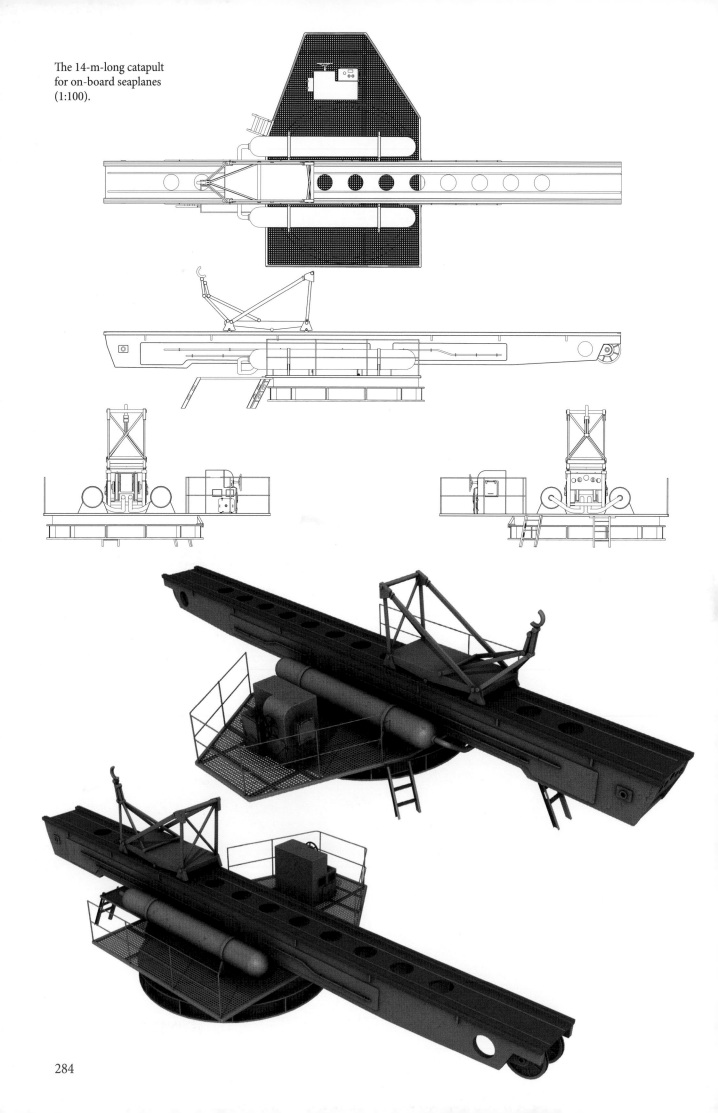

The 14-m-long catapult
for on-board seaplanes
(1:100).

Stereoscopic 3D visualizations
of *Scharnhorst*
– **Mariusz Motyka**